WORKING REMOTELY

Secrets to Success
for Employees on
Distributed Teams

Teresa Douglas
Holly Gordon
Mike Webber

© 2020 Teresa Douglas, Holly Gordon, and Mike Webber

Published by Kaplan, Inc., d/b/a Barron's Educational Series
750 Third Avenue
New York, NY 10017

www.barronseduc.com

10 9 8 7 6 5 4 3 2 1

ISBN: 978-1-5062-5433-3

Kaplan, Inc., d/b/a Barron's Educational Series print books are available at special quantity discounts to use for sales promotions, employee premiums, or educational purposes. For more information or to purchase books, please call the Simon & Schuster special sales department at 866-506-1949.

Printed in Canada

Acknowledgments

There were many people who helped move this book from an idea into reality, and we would like to thank them for their support. Jim Shevlin started this project in the first place, and then let us run with it. Lola Disparte contributed hours of her time toward the writing and editing of this book. Paula Fleming took time off from her holidays to copy edit our writing so we would have a clean copy to submit for publication.

Caitlin Duke joined the team at the 11th hour and helped us write, organize, and edit the vignettes and pro tips in a very short amount of time. We wouldn't have made our deadline without her.

We would also like to thank all of the Kaplan colleagues, past and present, who contributed vignettes, pro tips, or personal experiences to our book. Thank you Corinne Simon, Ibrahim Husain, Christine Terrell, Dru Ciotti, Bobby Amirebrahimi, Brian Sabel, Evan Gaughan, Rei Champion, Walker Williams, Julie Minnich, Melanie McKay, Jenn Freeman, Yeo Ju Choi, Kristin Robinson, Sascha Strelka, Chrissy Damasco, Elle Mastenbrook, Dustin Semo, Patrick Reagan, Kate Mitsakis, Melody Young and Katie Stanfield. Sharing your personal experiences helped us to create a book that is truly by employees, for employees.

A big thank you to the team at 750 Publishing for their flexibility and willingness to nurture this book and help it see the light of day.

TABLE OF CONTENTS

Before You Begin

In midsummer 2010, I received a strange call from my manager. I was instructed to make myself available at 4:00 p.m. and to be in a place where I could talk freely without my fellow employees hearing. It was both mysterious and unsettling, but most of all it was intriguing.

When I dialed into the rather large conference call, I realized the presenter was the much-admired CEO of our division. His first words were galvanizing: "If you are not able to keep a secret, please leave this call immediately." And so it began.

The next hour was spent detailing an audacious plan to completely shift the current business model for Kaplan Test Prep, the world's leader in the field.

On November 3, 2010 (just a few months from that midsummer call), Kaplan would essentially flip a switch and change from a brick-and-mortar organization, with 170 physical locations throughout the United States, Canada, and Europe, to a predominantly virtual company where almost 90 percent of all employees would work from home. While on the surface Kaplan would continue to service students as it always had, the organizational structure behind that service would transform completely.

—Jim Shevlin

That provides the background for this book. On a single day in 2010, a 70-year-old, industry-leading company completely embraced the remote workforce and implemented an entirely new organizational structure. Written after the fact, this book is about the lessons learned from that extreme transformation—by employees, for employees.

This book is about being a remote worker, from the perspective of remote workers. By detailing the many lessons we learned transitioning from traditional offices to remote ones, we hope to help others understand how to enter, enjoy, and thrive in the wonderful world of working from home (or a library, or a coffee shop, or an exotic island). We have tried to write honestly and directly about the physical aspect of this type of work. We have tried to portray the mental challenges of this job. But most importantly, we have tried to provide words to convey the extraordinarily novel emotional and psychological considerations of working within this structure.

The main thrust of this book is not about how to manage a remote workforce—at least, not directly. As their titles clearly indicate, many of the books available today about working remotely are focused, with varying levels of success, on this management challenge. But while this book is not primarily about how to manage remote workers, we believe it is a tremendous resource for managers because of what it *does* discuss: the remote worker, from the remote worker's perspective. To manage remote employees, a manager needs to understand remote employees. In fact, the last section of this book is written specifically for managers, but it will only be completely understood by a manager who has incorporated the lessons from the earlier chapters.

The biggest revelation we experienced while researching this book was that, thus far, little consideration has been given to the thoughts and emotions of the remote employee; the psychology of the remote worker is rarely addressed. But, by definition, a remote worker must confront a number of challenges alone. As we began to structure this book, we realized we had to focus on the psychological world of the remote employee as a definitive element of the experience. Only by understanding this inner world of the mind could the reader make sense of the corresponding physical and functional aspects of working remotely.

This book is written by the employees who made it through Kaplan's radical transformation and thrived. By writing about an experience that is based on the collective realities of many brilliant and sharing individuals, we hope to portray a picture of what could and should be the reality for future remote workers everywhere.

By employees, for employees. Let's begin the journey.

Chapter 1

Secrets of the Right Mentality

Of all the transitions you'll have to make as you move from a traditional office into the remote workforce, the psychological adjustments may be the most surprising. Many people already know that they need a comfortable physical workspace. This section will help you think about setting up a comfortable mental space as well.

Settling into Your New Environment

Working in a remote environment is something that you may not have experienced before. There are many similarities between working remotely and working in a more traditional office setting, but there are also many differences. When you're a virtual employee, you shoulder more responsibility to understand your company's culture and ensure you are living up to your commitments.

What do you really know about the company you work for? When you started, what kind of research did you do? If its stock is publicly traded, did you check its performance on the stock exchange? Did you do an internet search of the company name along with keywords like "love," "good employer," and "quit"? Doing this type of investigative work before signing on with a company gives you both a sense of job security and some context for the information your interviewers provide. Gone are the days of a job for life. The best and brightest will likely work for several companies, so it's important to control that process to be in charge of your career. Investigating potential employers is crucial.

Far too often, this investigation, if it occurs at all, ceases once someone accepts a job offer. This makes sense in the short term—after all, the interview was a success, the new job is yours, and if you did that important research before accepting the position, you probably feel that you know enough about the company to rest easy about your decision and how your new role fits with your long-term goals.

In reality, though, you don't know enough about the company. You may know the likelihood of its longevity over the next few years, but you have no idea about the inner workings of the different departments you'll soon be interacting with, what your boss is really like, or why your colleague, who is supposed to be showing you the ropes, is acting in such a cold manner toward you.

In a traditional office environment, a lot of your knowledge about the company's history and culture occurs through a natural process of osmosis. You overhear conversations in the next cubicle. You run into a colleague on the way to the printer and take a few minutes to discuss why they look so frustrated. Lunch provides a great opportunity to learn the backstory of recent changes. While this can easily spill into gossip, it quickly provides a good understanding of why things are the way they are.

When you're part of a remote workforce, that intrinsic knowledge is much harder to come by. It will come eventually, but by the time you have a full picture of the company's history and its major and minor players, a significant amount of time will have passed (more than would have in a non-virtual work environment). There's no point in waiting that long and struggling unnecessarily as you start out. The solution is to take action.

If your company provides you with a relevant company history, it's an excellent sign of a company that cares. If you don't receive such a history, or the one you're provided is superficial at best, then it is up to you to obtain a history you can use. Ask for a summary of recent changes that affected the organizational structure of the company and your division. Ask for the background on any personnel changes that are relevant to you in your new position. Requests such as these are a big part of setting yourself up for success in the remote workforce.

Without this knowledge, you're going to be guessing at how to best perform your duties and maneuver among colleagues and departments. But there is more at risk than just that. As we'll discuss in later chapters, networking in the virtual work environment begins much earlier than in the traditional workplace. Knowing the lay of the land from the past to the present allows you to start mapping out your career right away and avoid falling into the hidden traps created by events that took place before you ever arrived.

If you are in the process of onboarding, you can ask your HR department if they have a video or a manual or other collateral that discusses the history of the company, including when your role or department went remote. If you are not in the process of onboarding, or your HR department doesn't have any materials, then you may be able to gain this information in other ways. You could informally ask people to share their stories—how did they get hired into the role they are in now, when did they join the company, etc. This activity will help you build a picture of recent company history, and help you build your network, all at once.

—Teresa Douglas

Knowledge and trust are keys to success as a member of the remote workforce. Know what you're getting into before signing on with a company, and know what you've gotten into once you're there. There is a baseline level of trust that every employer-employee relationship needs to have, but in a remote workforce, the stakes in this circle of trust are significantly higher. It is incumbent on you, the remote worker, to both understand the implications of this change and embrace the dynamics that now exist. Your company has given you freedom and responsibility, and you must understand both the opportunity and the trap that lie therein.

As you will discover, the world of working remotely can give you greater day-to-day autonomy, more control over your work-life blend, and a greater ability to craft your job in ways that you may have previously thought unimaginable. These are all exciting possibilities. Frankly, only time will tell whether you can do these things well while working from home. In the remote workplace, temptations are plentiful. You will need to manage yourself, internalizing the employer part of the contractual bargain and weighing each and every decision you make throughout the day as both employer and employee.

Until you begin to work remotely, it may be difficult for you to understand the extraordinary trust that your company has placed in you, and it may be hard for you to comprehend just how much effort and thought you will have to exert to understand the implications of that trust. As you begin (and continue) to work in the remote workforce, you must periodically ask yourself whether you are up to the challenge and determine whether you are fulfilling your duties.

It is not unheard of for people to agree to work remotely and then spend their days ignoring their responsibilities until their company inevitably lets them go. In a similar vein, not all managers thrive in this environment, where trust is crucial to success. A lack of trust often leads to micromanaging and, ultimately, the resignation or dismissal of the remote employee. However, these stories say much more about the individuals involved than they do about working remotely.

There are also many workers on the opposite end of the spectrum: those who fulfill all of their work obligations appropriately and use the flexibility remote work offers to lead a more abundant life. There are remote workers who train for marathons, foster children, and fulfill other life dreams they may not have been able to without the flexibility offered by remote work.

It is common for companies to be overcontrolling as workers migrate away from the office. It is equally common for remote workers to initially feel as though they are on the outside looking in as they get acclimated to new communication patterns and new logistical arrangements. Discuss these things openly and honestly with your manager and your peers alike. Work through your tentative feelings as you enter the new world.

Your company has gone all-in on your abilities, your maturity, and your discipline. Seize this opportunity. Fulfill the contract you have made. Build your particular remote existence within the parameters established by your company and reap the benefits that result.

Preparing to Work More

What kind of worker are you? Are you someone who looks for any job that gives you a decent salary? Are you after a particular line of work that you will enjoy, regardless of the financial benefits? Or maybe you want anything that keeps your evenings and weekends completely free. These are important questions to ask yourself before getting into the virtual workforce, because one thing is certain in this environment: You will work more.

This concept can be hard for people to grasp, as from the outside the assumption is that you have more free time. After all, there's no boss in the room to watch over you. You have fewer distractions from coworkers, fewer clients coming in with questions, and just less noise all around. But the reality is actually the opposite. With fewer outside distractions, the right type of worker can suddenly have eight hours of pure work time. It's amazing how much time gets used up with random interruptions that are commonplace in an on-site office environment. Once those are removed, all that is left is for you to work. Granted, there are other potential distractions, but it's important to understand that contrary to popular belief, working from home means working more.

Let's take a moment to consider your new workspace. You now have fewer reasons to get up to accomplish tasks. Things like walking across the hall to get supplies or to the copy room to get a printout are all but eliminated, as hard copies are rarely required when working remotely. In the event that you do need to print something, the printer is usually right next to you. Those couple of minutes spent on the move in a traditional office environment can turn into something much longer when they present the opportunity to run into a colleague or supervisor. Any situation involving leaving your desk—getting coffee in the break room, running a suggestion by your boss, heading to the conference room for a meeting—provides an opportunity for distraction. In the virtual workforce, most of these actions are done with a click or two of your mouse.

The other major difference is that when you work from home, it's much harder to separate your home life from your work life. You no longer go out into the world and enter a different building to start your workday. Instead, work is just . . . there. Switching off becomes much more challenging, and it can be easy to start earlier, finish later, and find yourself working on weekends. It becomes harder to tell yourself that things can wait when in the most literal sense, they don't have to—the computer is right there.

The tendency to work more in this environment isn't necessarily a terrible thing, but you need to recognize and manage it carefully to get the right level of satisfaction out of your job and your work-life blend. Ultimately, you have more freedom in how you work, so use that to your advantage. Schedule regular breaks in your routine: Set an alarm to remind yourself to get up and stretch, walk to a nearby coffee shop, or work on a craft project. The activity you choose is less important than the act of taking regular breaks. Just knowing you have a 10-minute break in your day to do something you enjoy can keep you happy and productive in your role.

 When you work remotely, your office is really wherever you and your laptop are. I've learned that this makes my technological boundaries just as important as physical ones in a typical office. For example, I don't have my work email go directly to my phone, allowing my phone to remain a personal device while my laptop is a work device. This helps me to feel unplugged when my work laptop is closed, and sends a clear signal that I'm only available for urgent needs when I've shut down my computer for the day.

—Christine Terrell

Identifying what you want out of your virtual workforce job will help establish a base level of satisfaction. Know that you will be working more and recognize what that is: an opportunity. It's an opportunity to immerse yourself more fully in exciting work with fewer distractions than you might experience while working in an office. You can take great satisfaction in helping your colleagues and clients in a more timely and efficient manner and make your job something more than just a 40-hour-a-week way to keep the wolf from the door.

At the same time, recognize that this is a double-edged sword you need to wield wisely. Schedule breaks for yourself and set limits so you don't end up burning out. Walk into this working situation with eyes wide open, being prepared to both work more and reap the benefits of doing so.

Dealing with Reactions of Friends and Family

A month or so after I started working from home, I began getting calls from my mother in the middle of the day. At first I was concerned. We lived on different coasts, and a call in the middle of my workday used to mean that something momentous had happened. Someone was in a car accident, or sick, and I needed to either buy a plane ticket or call a relative in the hospital.

These turned out not to be those kind of calls. My mom missed having me nearby and thought that I would now have time to chat. I would gently let her know that I was in the middle of my workday, but it would still take 45 minutes to get off of the phone, and she would forget and call me again the next time she thought of it.

I found that the only solution was to not pick up the phone during work hours. She always left a message, and I could listen to it right away and decide if I needed to call back immediately. If not, I made a note to call her in the evening when I had time to talk. Gradually the midday phone calls stopped, and we went back to our regular routine of talking after my business day was done.

—Teresa Douglas

No one really understands what other people do for work. We have a much better idea about traditional jobs, the ones children are taught about in school: police officer, nurse, construction worker. But even with those jobs, it can be hard to picture what really happens. When do police file paperwork? How do nurses structure their days? What do construction workers actually do, when so much of their job appears to consist of standing about, waiting? It's not a surprise, then, that it's hard to visualize what a claims adjustor or regional sales director does day to day. Now take that confusion and multiply it by a factor of 10. Welcome to the way friends, family, and even some coworkers view the life of a remote worker, regardless of the job title.

Your home is your place of rest. It's where you raise your family, where you do chores on weekends, where you watch TV and relax. Adding business to the mix, even if you have a designated office area to work from, complicates things. It can be hard for even the person working remotely to figure it all out, so it makes sense that others have a hard time understanding where the line between work and non-work is. Confusion and questions from friends and family are understandable. Fortunately, the trick to navigating these conversations is straightforward: Anticipate questions and comments and take preemptive action, or at least be prepared to respond to the usual queries and misconceptions.

Many people will assume that because you're working from home, you are self-employed and therefore able to set your own hours and work as much or as little as you want. Being part of a remote workforce often means a significant amount of flexibility when it comes to your working hours, but not to the extreme that many people assume. Point out that you have a number of tasks to accomplish each day and that while some things can be moved around, most cannot unless you end up working late into the night to catch up.

Another common misconception is that when you tell an acquaintance you work from home, what that acquaintance hears is, "I'm in between jobs." Providing a bit more detail about your routine can clarify the situation, but having to justify your employment status can slowly wear away at a person's soul: "Trust me! I have a job! I swear it!" The sister reaction to this unemployment assumption is a kind of faux jealousy. This is where the person you're speaking with tells you how lucky you are to have such an easy gig, working from home. Again, a brief description of all that transpires in your day-to-day activities is often enough to educate the other person, but this assumption (like the unemployment one) can make you feel as though you're fighting an uphill battle.

It can be frustrating when friends don't understand your work situation, but it's not something that necessarily requires a lot of discussion. With family, however, it can become a more sensitive topic. A significant other or children living with you need to understand what working from home really means. At the same time, you need to accept that they are not likely to fully understand, so you need to be patient with them. To expect your family members to grasp right away why you can't spend part of the day doing housework or helping with homework is just inviting trouble. There's a flip side to this situation, of course. Working remotely may mean having the ability to arrange your schedule so you *can* take 30 minutes on your lunch break to vacuum. You *can* spend an hour in the evening finishing up work emails in order to spend an hour in the afternoon helping your son do his homework. But family should not assume this level of flexibility or conflict will likely arise.

Lay out the ground rules in advance to minimize confrontations and incorrect expectations. Set up your workplace and time so it's clear, for example, that when the door is closed, no one enters. That until the tie comes off, you're at work. That when the clock turns to 10:00 a.m., the workday begins. Control the expectations of those you live with, and your relationships will avoid dips into disappointment and frustration.

Ultimately, the answer is to be prepared. People who don't work remotely will never fully understand what it's like, and that's OK. You'll likely never know what it's like to be a police officer. In being prepared, however, you'll be better equipped to deal with the different situations you most certainly will encounter. As a bonus, after experiencing the misconceptions many friends and family members will have about working remotely, you're likely to presume a lot less about what the construction worker's average workday is like.

Overcoming Isolationism

Working remotely can be a lonely experience. Even if you are equipped with the secrets we are sharing, you'll likely experience a sense of isolation that can be both overt and covert in its effect on the human psyche. You don't feel the simple joy of stopping by a cubicle to chat with a friend or accidentally bumping into a colleague or high-level boss in an elevator. Even introverts may need interaction, however fleeting or trivial.

The volume of remote workforce decisions can overwhelm even the most diligent and organized person. It can be easy to think that no one in the company works as hard as you or that your team is the only competent one out there. You might lose sight of the big picture—or feel like you never had a grasp of the big picture in the first place. You might be surprised by sudden changes to your business unit or processes. Although not everyone who works from home experiences these extremities of emotion, those who do can feel them intensely.

So here is the secret to surviving these moments: Understand that you may occasionally be overcome by the isolation of the remote workforce life. Make your plan *now* to handle this psychological crisis, because we guarantee that if it does occur and you do not have a plan, you will not have the emotional gyroscope to finesse it when things start to go dark.

Build a support structure that you can lean on during tough times. The savvy remote worker ensures that structure includes people and actions both inside and outside of the company. Sometimes you need to speak to someone on the inside whose judgment you trust, either to vent or to ask for advice. Cultivate friendships now while things are going well so you know who you can talk to when times are rough. At other times, you need to remind yourself that there is a world outside of your home office. Consider joining a book club, or a professional association, or a game night at your local pub or library. Become a docent at your local museum. Volunteer on the weekends. If you have a pet or a hobby or a child, there is a good chance that there is a group out there of like-minded people who meet together socially. Try a few different things until you find your tribe and then attend regularly.

My team enjoys frequent virtual work-alongs that help us both stay connected socially and be more productive. If we anticipate that we will be doing similar work during a given week, we schedule a group video call to chit-chat and bounce ideas off each other while we work in parallel.

—Brian Sabel

Sometimes changing where you physically work can ward off feelings of isolation. It may not be as efficient to do some of your work at a local library or coffee shop, but the act of sitting in a room with other people may help you feel more connected to the world in general. If spending two hours at a library every Tuesday morning can keep you feeling energized about your job, then it is time well spent. Take some time on the weekends to try out new places (and check the Wi-Fi).

If your life circumstances and role allow for it, you might consider taking a class in the middle of the workday. Some employees find that taking time out for a group yoga or drawing class helps them fill the need for human contact.

If you find yourself in crisis mode despite all this, don't do anything rash. Breathe in and breathe out. Seek counsel from friends and family about the issue. Seek counsel from other remote workers. Go for a walk. Wait a preset period of time before making any career-changing decisions. You can opt out at any time, but once you do, it is very difficult to opt back in. We are not saying everyone can and will adapt to the world of working remotely. Many fine employees find that working from home is simply not a good fit. But we are saying you should not leave the remote workforce because of a predictable (and oftentimes transitory) wave of emotion.

Rely on your support network to weather the tough times. With the help of people and activities both inside and outside the company, you can experience the joys and flexibility that remote working provides for years to come.

Staying Engaged: How to Be Social

Connecting socially with your coworkers is a vital part of staying engaged in the remote workforce. But how do you connect socially when you're separated by screens and hundreds (or thousands!) of miles? You may think it's impossible to have any kind of workplace social life as a remote employee, but by using all the resources and technology available, your social interactions can be extremely beneficial and enjoyable.

From this moment forward, be intentional in your interactions. You will no longer walk past someone's office on the way to a meeting or run into them at the water cooler. These quick minutes here and there can build a strong foundation with coworkers. When working from home, the accidental meetings won't necessarily happen on their own, so you need to make them happen.

Take time to just say hello to your coworkers. If your company uses an instant messaging program, periodically use this technology to check in. If you would normally stop in and ask someone how their weekend was in the office, do the same on instant messenger. These interactions only take a couple of minutes, but they can make a big difference in your relationships with coworkers. It can be much easier to work with someone if a social structure is built outside of regular work interactions.

You can also do quick check-ins when you see someone mentioned in a mass email. Promotions, project successes, and even birthdays are often communicated via mass email. Take the extra minute to reach out to the people mentioned and congratulate them. Your support can go a long way.

Stay actively involved in all communication methods set up by your team. If there is a group email going around or a running group chat, participate in it. If there isn't, start one! Adding in a couple of thoughts here and there will not only help your team get to know you better but also help you feel more connected to your team. When you share your ideas, you will feel more involved and have a greater sense of satisfaction with your project work.

Video can be another great way to connect to your coworkers, so don't be afraid of it. Making sure you are always camera-ready from the waist up is a great way to be able to interact with coworkers on a moment's notice. Sometimes, seeing a friendly face is a huge morale booster. Being face-to-face also requires a greater amount of attention, as you likely will not be checking emails, walking around the house, or feeding the dog while video-chatting with someone. This increased attention leads to increased engagement and connection. Being fully present in communications with your coworkers can help them feel valued and show them you care.

There are many other ways to effectively use video with your coworkers. Scheduling time to meet as a group on video can have the same increased benefits as meeting one-on-one on video, combined with the positive effects of group conversation. These group interactions can happen in many different ways and with many different purposes. Work-along sessions are a great way to foster creative development, stay on track, and produce a large amount of work in a short amount of time. Typically, when in person, the focus of a work-along would be to brainstorm and think aloud. While this can happen in a virtual work-along as well, there's an opportunity for a different focus. It can be incredibly helpful to "sit" in a virtual meeting room and work on the same project—even if most of the time it is silent, save for the sound of typing. Not only can you feel more connected, knowing that everyone is in the same mental space working on the same project, but you can also get on your microphone and ask a quick question at any point. If you need an idea for what to write next, or you want the group's opinion on your next step, everyone is there working together. At the end of a work-along, your group will have a large amount of progress to show and celebrate since everyone was putting time and effort in together.

Speaking of celebrating, commemorating group accomplishments and life events can happen remotely just as they would in the office. If your team finishes a successful project, gather everyone on a video call to celebrate. You can even bring in high-level managers to the calls. It can help for these managers to see who was involved in specific projects and for the team to be introduced to the managers they may not have met.

Building connections with group video can happen outside the typical workday and project structure as well. Just as you may have participated in happy hours after work with colleagues, the same can happen in the virtual world, with many added benefits! It is cheaper when everyone can bring their own beverage, there's no risk of drinking and driving when everyone is sitting at their computer in their home, and any accidental uncomfortable physical interactions cannot take place.

On the flip side, it still has the same great benefits that meeting outside of work provides. You can get to know one another on a personal level, again building stronger connections that will improve your relationships inside and outside of work. You also have the ability to loosen up and be your true self. These opportunities are often taken for granted in the traditional office environment but can occur online as well. In fact, depending on the software used, interactions can be much more fun online. For instance, some video programs allow you to add fun backgrounds to your picture and even play games together. Just because you aren't physically in the same space as your coworkers doesn't mean you can't have fun with them.

While building connections in the remote workforce can take a little more effort on your part, these relationships are just as beneficial and necessary as those in physical offices. Participate in activities offered to you and take time to create your own. Over time, virtual interactions will become second nature, feeling just as natural as talking face-to-face.

Chapter 2

Secrets of the Outer and Inner Physical Environment

Working remotely means never having to put up with someone else's office layout. *You* are in total control. Here are some things to think about as you set up the workspace that's right for you.

The Physical Secrets for Ultimate Comfort

> *Changing my vantage point once a week helps bump up my productivity and gives me a variety of options to choose the most comfortable work environment. I'll relocate outside on nice days for a few hours, or visit a local coffee shop. The change in scenery is refreshing and helps keep me energized.*
>
> *I find that even moving to another location in my home can be helpful. When my day is winding down, I can move from my office desk to the couch to begin relaxing while I sort through the final tasks I need to accomplish.*
>
> —Evan Gaughan

One of the most underappreciated aspects of working remotely is the very real time and cost savings. Consider your commute time to a traditional office. Let's say, for example, that your commute takes 30 minutes each way, twice a day. With an average of 240 workdays in the year, this equates to approximately 240 hours or 6 workweeks spent commuting. Then there are the additional monetary costs (gas for your car, fare for public transportation, etc.). Add bad weather, road rage, or an accident into the mix, and your commute can be the most stressful part of your day. For many remote workers, getting that commute time back is priceless.

Another benefit to working from home is the reduced wardrobe cost. While business casual or an actual uniform is standard in most workplaces, working remotely often offers you greater wardrobe flexibility. Obviously you still need to be presentable—and ready—for video calls. However, this can mean wearing a collared shirt with your jeans and slippers. Others keep a blazer ready to slip on over a T-shirt. Because your colleagues only see you from the shoulders up, it doesn't matter if you wear the same (clean) shirt over and over again. Of course, dressing for work comes with the benefit of building a routine and getting into the working mindset, but being remote allows you the flexibility to determine some of those standards for yourself. Also, if you only wear a suit jacket for a few hours a week, it lasts longer. This means fewer purchases throughout the year, and your lifetime, to maintain your wardrobe, which leads to additional savings.

Lunchtime is another opportunity where the remote worker can save considerable time and money. When working in an office, generally you're stuck with two options: packing a lunch or eating out. Packing a lunch requires planning, time, and remembering to take said lunch with you to work. Alternatively, if you venture out of the office in search of a reasonably priced option, you're racing against the clock and trying to balance your food budget, all while attempting to enjoy your "break" from work.

Working from home means never forgetting your lunch on the counter again. Full access to your fridge and kitchen also allows for greater control of the health and nutrition of your meals. Some remote workers have taken the opportunity to become locavores, while others have taken up bread making. You're limited only by your own imagination and culinary skills.

If you have children, then child care may also take a significant portion of your income. Depending on where you live, child care costs can potentially eat anywhere between 10 and 50 percent of your monthly salary. This doesn't include workdays lost to caring for sick children. Working remotely, however, offers much more flexibility in terms of the amount and type of child care needed. While this may or may not translate into actual dollars saved (though it likely will), it increases options for care and can allow for more time spent with your loved ones. Some parents have (with their manager's approval) crafted a split schedule—adding a weekend day or some early morning and late evening hours into their work schedules so they can care for their children for a portion of the day. This schedule flexibility has helped some reduce the amount of child care they need to pay for, while others have eliminated this cost entirely through the strategic use of family and friends.

Without a doubt, working from home can add both money and time back into your daily routine. This is but the tip of the iceberg. Take a look at your workflow and get creative. With a little thought, you will soon have the kind of work-life balance that makes you the envy of your friends.

Your Workspace

When you work remotely, not only *can* you have your office the way you want—you *should* have your office the way you want. It needs to be set up in a way that will allow you to be a productive worker. The space should be distinctive for you, clearly identifying itself (to you and to others) as your workspace. This is important because there need to be boundaries that differentiate the space you work in from the space you live in. Where you live is typically your place of rest, a location you don't associate with the outside world, where family and non-work activities traditionally take place. Working from home means carving out a section of your living space and converting it into a working space, both physically and mentally.

Ideally, your home office is a separate room with a door you can close. If you aren't able to devote an entire room to your workspace, consider taking the time to arrange the furniture in a way that creates a clear division between the space where you work and the space where you live. If having a permanent space dedicated to working is not realistic, you can still make your space work-ready by having a routine at the start of your day where you adjust the furniture and lighting and bring your tools for the day out from a cupboard. The end of your workday can consist of your morning routine in reverse, transforming your space back into your personal living environment. It's also wise to avoid lumping your personal "work" tasks and your actual work tasks together in the same space. Ideally, you should not do your taxes or pay your bills in your non-personal work area. Another benefit of having a defined workspace at home is that you may qualify for tax deductions for a dedicated home office. You may wish to consult a tax expert to see if this is true for your home and financial situation and to find out what the government requires to claim the deduction.

There are a few physical items every home office needs in order to function, mainly a good desk and a good office chair. These ingredients are integral to the comfort and success of your work environment, and there is no one-size-fits-all solution. Every chair fits different people differently, and every desk has its strengths and weaknesses.

The best approach to finding your fit is to try different options. Try out multiple chairs, sit (or stand) at every desk you come across, and determine what you need from each. Consider whether you want (and have space for) multiple workspace configurations. For example, perhaps you want to spend part of your day working from a standing desk. Explore all options, keeping nothing off limits. When you find the right setup, be willing to invest in it. You'll likely be spending a lot of time using it, and just like a mattress or car, you want to make sure it is right for you.

I recommend putting together a mobile office. I have a big command-center style setup for my regular office as well as a scaled-down version of everything I need that fits easily in a backpack. That way, I can do big projects that require a lot of hardware at my home base, but I also have the option to easily hit the road and still get everything done. I prefer cloud storage solutions like Google Drive over saving files on a particular computer so that I always have access to them.

—Walker Williams

Once you have the basics down, it's time to build your surrounding workspace. As a remote worker, you'll likely spend some time on camera, so it's important that your face be properly lit. Consider a flexible desk light, one that can be turned to light your face as necessary to create a professional appearance on camera. Every aspect of your lighting is within your control—make it work for you.

The décor of your office can paint a picture in your coworkers' minds of who you are and how you work. Be cognizant of the items behind you while you are on camera. Some companies may have guidelines that dictate what should be seen. If your company has such guidelines, follow them. If not, pay attention to the workspaces of your coworkers. Often, following the lead of your colleagues is a good rule of thumb. Even if you are used to whatever is behind you, keep in mind that the person you are calling may not be, and if there is too much going on, it can be distracting. In most cases, keeping it simple is best.

Just as the items behind you can be distracting, so can the items in front of you. Find a view that allows you to maintain focus during your workday. For example, some people work best with a desk facing a wall that allows for full focus when at the computer. Others like to set up their workspace to allow them to look out a window.

Consider the ambience of your workspace. Do you enjoy working to music? If so, it would be worth your time to research radio or internet-streaming solutions to improve your work ambience. Also consider the atmosphere: Think temperature, air quality, and outside noise. Do you need a space heater? What about a desk fan? Maybe a couple of plants to increase the oxygen around you?

You may find that when choosing items to design your workspace, you wonder whether a certain purchase is superfluous. Art, fancy ergonomic furniture, and other items often make this list. As many remote workers will agree, though, you should allow yourself to spend more on the right items (for you). Your workspace is your home for a significant portion of each day. Investing in your comfort and enjoyment while working is truly a case of care of the soul.

Is there a pet in your home? The companionship throughout your workday can be beneficial, but thinking through the logistics is vital to making this work. Set up a space for pets that allows them to be near you while not interfering with your work. Be sure that a system is in place to keep everyone safe from electronics and cords. While some colleagues or clients may enjoy visits from animals, others may not. To be ready for a video call at any time with pets in the room or nearby, have a quick way to turn off your camera and mute your microphone. For example, if you know your dogs will bark at the mail carrier, putting up a gate may not be enough to keep them from disrupting a meeting.

The final thing to consider about your workspace is how to effectively take advantage of the flexibility that working remotely offers. Even if you love your home office, you may want to take advantage of working from a coffee shop sometimes. Or perhaps you have to be elsewhere for family or personal reasons. On a beautiful spring day, you might want to work from your patio. You may be someone who flourishes around other people; in that case, research coworking spaces in your area. On the other hand, some people, without the structure of their clearly defined office space, get easily distracted and find themselves being unproductive. Test the waters to see what your limitations are. Maintain your routines of how you log in and in what order you complete tasks, making these function as the structure of your working environment.

Working *from* home doesn't have to mean working exclusively *at* home. Keep things as separate as you can, both in terms of not working in the space where you live and not living in the space where you work. Nothing is set in stone: When you find things that work well for you, stick with them. If you come up with ideas to improve your workspace, implement them. Mix things up within your workspace to get the maximum value from being part of the remote workforce. Ultimately, your experience working remotely will be not only more tailored to how you work best but also far more enjoyable than any "perfect" on-site office ever was.

Your Tools

It's important to have the right tools for your job. Some tools are so crucial that they are necessary for you to do any work at all, whether in a traditional office or a remote one. When working remotely, the onus is often on you to ensure you are set up with all the tools you need.

Your company may provide a computer. In such a case, you will likely be restricted as to what programs you can put on the machine and have little to no choice about whether the computer is a laptop or a desktop and what operating system it uses. However, you typically don't have to pay for the device or the software. Alternatively, you may have the option to use your own computer, allowing you greater latitude for customization.

Of all your tools, a computer is likely the one you will use the most in your job, so it's important to have it set up in a way that allows you maximum comfort and efficiency. If the monitor is too small, definitely consider upgrading (assuming that such a change does not go against any company policy). A few other things to consider adding include an external keyboard and mouse, an external webcam, an external microphone, and headphones. While this list is not exhaustive, it should give you a sense of the importance of choosing the right technology for your situation.

To the extent that you are allowed, install the programs that you like best. Use the browser you feel most comfortable with and the email client you prefer. Customize other programs so they look and behave the way you like, with your frequently used features readily accessible.

While you may be able to do some work without an internet connection, access to online resources is generally essential. Even if you can complete all or some of your work in an offline program, that work often needs to be transferred to or from somewhere online. Therefore, a fast, reliable internet connection is necessary for most tasks in the remote world. Where possible, choose an internet provider with a good reputation and educate yourself on bandwidth and connection speeds. Depending on the type of remote work you do, you may need a wired connection. Many remote employees need to attend regular video meetings, and a wired connection is more consistent than a wireless one, reducing the risk of freezes and call failures. This becomes even more crucial when dealing with clients. Colleagues may be willing to work through your technical challenges, but a client will likely find the overall presentation and service lacking, and this may affect their desire to stay with your company. Therefore, if you are allowed to choose your own computer, make sure you get one with an Ethernet port if necessary.

Don't take for granted all the resources that come with working in a traditional office building. You may need various supplies to do your job remotely. If you work with paper, do you have a printer and spare ink cartridges? Pencils, paper clips, and a stapler could also be essential. Do you have a way to store important documents? USB drives, cameras, and other electronic equipment might also be items you use every day. Your company may have a list of items you are expected to keep on hand. If so, use this resource. If not, when setting up your office space, consider what you need and prepare the space accordingly.

It's essential that you take care of your tools. Clean your computer regularly, both the outer surface and its hard drive. A computer that is regularly maintained performs better than one that is not. Deleting temp files, defragmenting the hard drive, and cleaning the desktop will help keep your computer from slowing down. Check with your company's IT department, as some performance-boosting tasks may be done automatically, while others may need to be done manually. If the latter is the case, set reminders as appropriate so you can do these maintenance tasks.

You should also be prepared in case one of these important tools fails. Back up your computer on a regular basis so that all your data are not lost if your hard drive crashes. If your internet goes down, know where to go to get online again as quickly as possible. Your phone may be able to function as an internet hotspot to bridge a temporary outage. If your documents are in the cloud and you have mobile versions of the necessary apps on your phone or tablet, you may be able to work on your mobile device, at least for a while. Arm yourself in advance with the know-how to access the content you need on your mobile device and any additional costs for going online through your carrier. It's also a good idea to have a colleague's phone number on hand in cases where you can't easily get back online. You may have important meetings or tasks to complete, and that colleague can let others know what's going on. Being prepared for this situation will reduce your stress and the negative impact on others if it does occur.

I showed up 10 minutes early to a video call I was running to get the virtual room set up, load the PowerPoint deck, and chat with the attendees as they came in. Approximately one minute before the session was supposed to start, my screen went dark. It took a few minutes to figure out that I'd lost power, and with it, my connection to the internet. I grabbed my mobile office bag, stuffed my computer and power cord into it, texted my boss to tell the team what had happened, and rushed to the coffee shop six blocks away, where I was sure to have power and Wi-Fi.

While it was frustrating to have to use my plan B, I was sure glad I knew exactly where to go, and how to communicate, when I couldn't use my workspace as intended.

—*Teresa Douglas*

Treat all your tools with the respect they deserve and be prepared for any situation in which you lose one of them. Your mastery of the nuances of the remote working environment will help you to maximize your productivity.

Your Physical Fitness

> *I am passionate about fitness and making connections with my colleagues, two pursuits that can be challenging in the remote environment. To keep myself accountable, I created an online Health & Wellness Community in which my co-workers and I post recipes, fitness tips, mindfulness ideas, and even funny memes. I lead the group and post once or twice a week, which encourages virtual water cooler talk. We also commit to challenges ranging from posting pictures of our go-to healthful lunches to running races out in the real world.*
>
> —Julie Minnich

You may have heard someone say that "sitting is the new smoking." As our lifestyles become more convenient, getting through the day makes fewer demands on our bodies. In our personal lives, we have smart devices that take care of everything from banking to grocery shopping with just the tap of a screen. In our work lives, many of us spend the majority of our day sitting in front of a computer. This is true whether you work in a traditional office or as part of the remote workforce. When we think about the challenges of working from home, we may focus on psychological issues and how to deal with them—situations that involve family, job satisfaction, and the need to connect with others. However, your physical health is just as important, and there is a lot that you can do to control the situation.

The first step toward managing your physical health in the remote workplace is to recognize that you need to actively manage your physical routine. Eliminating the commute to and from work also eliminates some exercise opportunities. Consider the extra steps you get when you commute into the city and work at an office. You might have to walk to the bus, or climb up and down stairs at the train station. If you drive, you have to park your vehicle at a lot and then walk into your office building. Your office might have stairs. The lunchtime food run provides another opportunity for activity as you walk a couple of blocks down the street and then back again. In a traditional office, you have to get up to walk down the hall for meetings or to use the photocopier. After work, you might walk to a pub or coffee shop with a couple of colleagues. All of these built-in movement opportunities go away when you work from home. That doesn't mean that remote workers must resign themselves to being less physically active. It simply means that you'll need to create those opportunities yourself.

Use the greater flexibility of working from home to your advantage. Build exercise time into your routine. Naturally, always check with your doctor before taking on new physical activities. Once you have the all-clear, there are several different things you can do to stay fit. Take advantage of flexibility in your schedule to arrange regular trips to the gym as appropriate. Some remote workers go to the gym in the afternoon, when there are fewer people on the machines, and then make up the work hours later in the evening. Other employees take a midmorning walk to get fresh air along with their exercise, while still others keep a set of weights near their desks. Do some research and try different things. Mixing up your fitness routine can also add variety to your day and help you manage your stress level.

You can also find fitness opportunities during work itself. Look into customizing your desk space to allow you to stand throughout the day (or for portions of it). This will improve your overall health and posture, while also strengthening your legs and back. You can purchase a standing desk, or you can do a little research into DIY standing options. Regardless of the route you go, changing your desk is much easier to do at home than in a traditional office, where company policy might prevent office workers from modifying their office spaces. Even if there is no such policy, some workers might feel uncomfortable about standing at their desks.

They might work in an open environment where standing will make them literally stand out amongst everyone else on the floor, and this can be embarrassing. That kind of social anxiety doesn't exist when working from home, so you can protect your health and your dignity all at once.

Consider other modifications beyond a standing desk. You could use an exercise ball instead of a chair, a pedal machine that allows you to keep your legs active while working, or even a treadmill desk. With a little research and some due diligence to prevent injury, you can leverage your remote working situation to be as healthy as possible.

Remind yourself to get up and take mini breaks throughout the day. In an office, you likely had to get up to retrieve documents, talk to colleagues, grab coffee, and go to meetings. At home, make excuses to get up periodically to stretch your legs and move around. Some workers even set a timer to remind themselves to get up at regular intervals throughout the day. You can also do a little research and find exercises you can do while sitting at your desk, for those days when it isn't possible to take an extended break.

Remember: Losing the traditional office doesn't have to mean losing all activity from your day. With a little thought and creativity, you may find that you have even more time to exercise than you did before.

Chapter 3

Secrets of Logistics

Most jobs have a certain rhythm for deliverables, such as calling all clients by the end of the day or closing out the accounts by the last day of the month. This section will help you set up the structure for the things you need to do.

How to Find What Works for You

> I work a flex schedule, which gives me a strong start in the form of early mornings and the opportunity to connect with my children throughout the day. While uninterrupted time can be built into any workday, it's an automatic part of all my days. I start work before most of my coworkers come online, which allows me quiet time to get a head start on the day's tasks or focus on a special project before email and chat notifications start popping up.
>
> Having this flexible schedule also lets me split child care with my husband. While I am working in the morning, he feeds our kids breakfast and prepares them for school. Before they head off, I get to hug them and occasionally help with a hairdo before continuing on with my work.
>
> I take a midafternoon break to retrieve my kids from school and get to hear about their day on the way back. Once we get home, I hand them off to the nanny and dive back into work.
>
> —Melanie McKay

Employees in the remote workforce can be very different from one another when it comes to how they manage their schedules. Some thrive by working all day, starting early in the morning and finishing late at night, with extended breaks scattered throughout. Others prefer a standard 9-to-5 workweek, with weekends off limits. To be a successful remote employee, you need to understand both your own preferences and the amount of flexibility you have in your role. There are many factors to consider when figuring out what works best for you while meeting the needs of your employer.

Start with considering the needs of the business. After all, if you can't do what is required to make your work a success for your employer, then you should probably be in a different position or perhaps even at a different company. The business you're in may have certain peak times every day or week, and you should be present for them. If you're on Pacific time and the majority of your clients and colleagues are on Eastern time, you are likely going to have to wake up early some days. If you're expected to talk to clients in the evening after they have finished work, then you'll need to include evenings in your working hours. Knowing the ebb and flow of your company's work rhythms will allow you to build your schedule accordingly, leading to professional success.

Once you have a solid idea of the rhythm of the business as a whole, take time to confirm expectations—both explicit and implicit—with your manager. For example, are people in your role expected to be available on the weekends? It does you no good to arrange your workweek in a way that works for you if your boss is not on board with it. Your manager may have certain expectations when it comes to daily or weekly meetings, or how you sign in and out. Your boss's own schedule preferences may also require you to be accessible at certain points in the day. This doesn't mean you'll have no say in these expectations; any good boss will want to meet the needs of remote employees where possible. Treat your schedule as an ongoing dialogue among you, your manager, and the needs of the business and be prepared for it to evolve over time.

With this knowledge as a foundation, you can confidently address your personal schedule preferences. When are you most productive? If you do your best thinking in the morning, then it makes sense to start your day early. Do you lose focus around midafternoon? Perhaps you need to schedule an extended break and return to work in the evening, when you have your second wind.

Some remote employees enjoy working during these traditionally "off" hours because with fewer people working, they can focus on a specific task. Alternatively, if you prefer to power through your day with very small breaks, then a more compact schedule is likely best for you.

Expect that your preferences may evolve over time. This is especially true if you have never worked remotely before. Once you have figured out the needs of your employer and the business, try out different schedules. Do a test and see what results in the highest levels of both productivity and personal satisfaction. This kind of experimentation is also useful because the company may need you to be flexible. Besides having peak hours of the day or days in the week, your company may have peak seasons, when you'll have to change your schedule to handle the extra load. Being too rigid with your schedule can cause more frustration than it prevents. While it is good to have a general structure to your day, remember to build in unstructured time for the unplanned events that always seem to crop up.

Many people talk about work-life blend; the remote workforce offers, in many cases, greater control over this blend. If you carefully consider the needs of your employer, your manager, and yourself as you construct your schedule, your experience in the virtual working environment will be a positive one. The beauty is that often those three stakeholders are very much in alignment with each other—it just takes some active consideration to find the perfect fit.

To my surprise, this practice has even made me more productive. That end-of-day deadline forces me to get everything crossed off my list by a specific time rather than dragging it out into the evening or next morning.

Your Daily Routine

> *When I first began to work remotely, it was difficult*
> *for me to end my day at a reasonable hour. I needed*
> *to re-create leaving my work on a computer halfway*
> *across town! I learned to actually schedule the end of each*
> *day in my calendar. At the appointed time, I wish my team*
> *a good evening, close the team chat client, use a separate*
> *browser so that I don't receive any more notifications, and*
> *stop all work-related activity.*
>
> —Brian Sabel

If you look at books on raising children, you'll find that the good ones nearly always talk about the importance of routine. It's a big new world for toddlers, and routine creates a sense of security, along with the opportunity to learn through the repetition of different processes. One might think that as adults, we no longer need this tool to survive different and new situations, but we're not that far removed from our younger selves. Just as taking those first steps and being away from mom can be a hard time for a small child, entering the remote workforce can feel equally traumatizing if you're not prepared for it.

We've already talked about the importance of creating boundaries to separate our work life from our home life. The next step is to look at our daily tasks and come up with a process that can be repeated and creates structure. In many cases, it doesn't actually matter what your routine consists of, just as long as one exists.

For most people, starting work each day at the same time will provide a strong foundation for a routine. You may not need to start work at, say, 9:00 a.m., and the ability to start working whenever is convenient for you is a huge benefit for some who work remotely. It can be tempting to sleep in on days when you don't have to meet people right away or complete time-sensitive tasks. That, however, is an advantage you should explore once your routine has been solidified and you are comfortable in the remote workforce. Until then, choosing a start time and sticking to it will provide you with a strong sense of consistency and ground you for the tasks you need to complete throughout the week.

Another approach that works for some people is to avoid checking email as the first task of the day. Email is like oxygen for most people who work remotely: We need it to function and survive. The problem is that many people in the virtual workforce get a high volume of email, and if you work with colleagues and clients who are in different time zones, your inbox in the morning can be quite full. If you check your email first thing, you run the risk of completing tasks in the order in which they appear in your inbox, rather than in order of importance. Over time, that kind of experience can be incredibly draining.

Instead of making your inbox your first stop, it may be more beneficial to have a list of tasks that you need to accomplish that set you up for your day, provide you with a sense of what's new, and allow you to cross off certain to-dos before they lose out to the temptation of working through a full inbox. Depending on your role, these tasks could include looking at the stock market, checking daily company updates, starting the apps you'll use throughout the day, checking in with colleagues, or listening to your voicemail. Your to-do list should be planned the day before or be a regular series of steps built into your routine. Some remote employees have no choice but to check email as one of the first steps in their day. If that describes your role, then you will need to build in a different type of discipline into your morning. Identify those messages that are directly related to the task at hand and mark them for immediate action; leave the remainder to be read and processed later in the day. In this fashion, email sets up your day but doesn't dictate it.

Building in routines later in the workday is also important. Try to take your lunch break at a regular time and for a consistent length of time. Planning smaller (but still deliberate) breaks is also wise—perhaps an afternoon tea, a power nap, or a walk around the block. Such breaks are not just time away from work but also regular activities that have the ability to become habits, giving you consistency throughout your week, every week. Taking a break and chatting with friends or surfing the internet can give you a breather from your work tasks, but unless you have a lot of structure and repetition to these breaks, they won't necessarily strengthen your routine.

It is also important to end the day at a regular time. Finishing at 5:00 or 6:00 p.m. makes sense for many people, as it means they stop working in time for dinner. The specific end time doesn't matter though, as long as it's generally consistent from day to day. In the remote workforce, it can be difficult to stop working. While at an office, you typically have to leave at some point, at home you never do. There is almost always something more to do, and your work space is always available to you. Having a planned end time to your day is essential for creating stability through routine.

Sometimes setting a planned end time is not enough to pull you away from work. If you have nothing to do in the evening, it can be easy to continue working after you had planned to stop. One way to break this habit is to schedule some activity immediately after work, such as spending time with a loved one, reading a book, eating dinner, or doing yoga. Plan something that you enjoy so that you are motivated to go do it. Creating a routine that helps you leave work— both physically *and* mentally—is vital for anyone who wants to enjoy working remotely.

Building a routine is important for both short-term and long-term success. Sometimes the excitement of a new world can mean that your enthusiasm overshadows the basic need for structure in your day. Suddenly you're a few weeks or months into your new virtual work experience and feeling overwhelmed. By setting a routine from the start, you can avoid the crash when the initial excitement wears off. Situations will come up that require you to vary your routine from time to time, but under this system, they will simply become the odd exception, rather than the way you live your working life.

How to Set Up Your Day

Remote employees often live and die by their calendars, and with good reason: Careful management of your schedule will allow you to be successful in your remote role. There are many calendar programs out there, but your company may require that you use a specific one. None of that really matters as long as you get in the habit of using your calendar to structure how you go about your daily tasks. Otherwise, you run the very real risk of missing deadlines or appointments. You may have heard mixed stories about productivity in the remote workforce. Some people say that they get more done as remote workers, while others have seen their productivity drop off. The difference between success and failure starts with a strategic approach to setting up your day.

Be aware of what lies ahead today, tomorrow, and into next week. Begin your day by checking your calendar. Look ahead and see whom you need to speak with and what preparations you need to make in advance of those meetings. The flow of each day—the balance of meeting time versus task time—will likely vary. Check your calendar regularly to keep up with the flow and to avoid showing up to a meeting at the wrong time or unprepared. Finally, toward the end of your workday, check what's happening tomorrow. Leave yourself a bit of time when you do this; too often, you'll see an early morning task or meeting that requires some advance preparation, and you can wind up working well past your planned end time. Give yourself enough of a cushion to prepare for tomorrow's schedule before today ends.

As you review your schedule for the next day, plan out the tasks and goals you need to complete and then build that time into your calendar. Give yourself deadlines. Don't assume that your tasks will somehow get done at some point in the day. If you haven't allotted time for those tasks on your calendar, it is all too easy for regular meetings, email, last-minute calls, and unexpected delays to fill your work hours. Use your schedule to determine what you do and when.

Don't forget to look at your workday as a whole. Do you have the right balance between scheduled work time devoted to specific tasks and unscheduled work time that can be used for meetings and other work? If you schedule too much task time, people may not be able to find time to meet with you on important issues. If you schedule too little task time, you may not have enough time to complete everything you have to do. When you first create your daily routine, you will have to use trial and error to find the right balance. Once you have been in your routine for a while, you can use experience to decide whether the ratio of task time to meeting time needs adjustment. If you feel overwhelmed by your workload, that may be a sign that you need to schedule more private work time and fewer meetings into your calendar.

Remember that other people's schedules will also have a direct impact on your calendar. A boss who spends most of his afternoons in meetings will likely be available for questions only in the morning, so plan for that situation. Alternatively, you may need to leave evenings free to make outbound calls to clients. For many in the remote workforce, time zones add further complexity to scheduling meetings and workload. When you start working with colleagues in different time zones, finding an appropriate meeting time can feel like a big task. With a little practice, however, you will soon become adept at finding a time that works for most. Find out which (and how many) time zones you have to contend with. Use this information to arrange your schedule so you can be available to colleagues during their work hours. Many calendar programs allow you to view the availability of colleagues on the same network. If the program allows it, enter in your usual business hours so your coworkers know whether they are trying to schedule a meeting outside your work hours. In this way, you can efficiently craft your schedule so that you are in sync with the people you work with the most.

It's equally important to schedule a proper lunch break and other breaks into your day. Just as important tasks can get swept aside if they aren't built into your calendar, lunchtime can easily disappear under the weight of your to-do list. The same goes for breaks. Sitting at your desk and working on the computer all day is not a healthy long-term strategy; you need moments to stretch your legs, get a drink, or go for a short walk outside. These breaks should be part of your regular day. They may not occur at the same time every day, and you may have some days with more time than others, but breaks are an important part of thriving in the remote workforce. Build them into your calendar and consider their timing: A mid-afternoon walk could be the perfect time to get your second wind as the day winds down. Make your lunch break an early or late one depending on the needs of the business so you're available for others as required at an appropriate time. Perhaps schedule another short break when your kids come home from school so you can say hello to them before diving back into work.

I used to feel guilty setting aside time during typical working hours to run to the post office or pop over to the store to get that missing ingredient for dinner, but that changed when I heard a senior colleague talk about getting his hair cut on a Tuesday afternoon because that was when he could fit it into his schedule.

I feel refreshed when I take time to get out of my house at least once a week. Since many of us start early, eat at our desks, and work after hours, taking breaks during the day for personal tasks is sometimes necessary. So long as I keep these personal task breaks to a minimum and complete them efficiently, I no longer feel guilty for making time in my calendar for them around my work responsibilities.

—*Jenn Freeman*

Working from home will likely cause your personal and professional calendars to overlap and become one. You may have the flexibility to take an afternoon off to catch a child's baseball game or get a massage. If you commit to something outside of work, schedule it into your work calendar so that nothing gets scheduled during the event. The reverse is also true: You need to schedule the time you plan to be working so that the other people in your life know you will be busy. By letting those who rely on you know when you are working and those you work with know when you are off, you will manage the expectations of all the people in your life while maintaining the balance you need.

You are in charge of managing your calendar efficiently. Just as a car needs an occasional tune-up to work well, your daily routine will function at maximum efficiency if you take the time to fine-tune your calendar. Take a look at the meetings on your calendar. Does every meeting have a purpose? Some meetings may be required by your supervisor, others may cover current projects, and still others may help your professional development. Avoid unnecessary meetings by learning how to say no. Saying no does not mean pushing something into the future; the future quickly becomes the present and those delayed meetings arrive before you know it. If your presence at a meeting is unnecessary, speak up! Talk to your supervisor about any meeting requests you feel uncomfortable turning down on your own. If there are valid reasons for you to decline the invite, your supervisor can work with you on next steps.

Of course, taking meetings off your calendar may not be possible. In that case, you can focus on making your non-meeting time as efficient as possible. It can take between 15 and 30 minutes to refocus after an interruption, so try to schedule your meetings in blocks, with small stretch breaks in between. Some employees designate a few days per week as their dedicated meeting days and spend the other days working exclusively on their task lists. Other employees schedule all their meetings in the afternoon, leaving the mornings free for work. If you can't do either of these things, try to schedule your meeting blocks far enough apart that you have one to two hours of private work time in between. This gives you the time you need to refocus and make progress on your task before the next meeting.

Remain flexible—understand that your calendar isn't set in stone. There will be days when four of your five scheduled meetings get bumped back or canceled entirely. This can be a great opportunity to get a head start on tomorrow's task list—or to take a walk around the block to decompress. The reverse can also happen. Your boss could call a meeting during your lunch break or squarely in the middle of the non-meeting work time you blocked out for yourself. Be prepared to shuffle things accordingly.

Whether it's to make your day more efficient, to be available for colleagues and clients, or to get time for yourself to rest, use your calendar to structure your day. Remember, those in the remote workforce who are highly structured are the ones who are highly successful. With that said, don't be locked into your daily and weekly plan when things come up that require you to change. Assume that all will go as planned, but be prepared to develop a plan B when required. Knowing what your day holds for you and when you need to accomplish all that's on your plate will give you a stable foundation and ultimately lead to a higher degree of satisfaction with your work.

How to Manage Your Inbox

Email is a crucial aspect of the remote workforce. In many instances, it is the only contact you will have with some of your coworkers and clients. Thus, the image you portray in your email can be the only image people have of you. As with handling other aspects of working virtually, managing email is best done by creating a system that works for you.

When working remotely, you'll likely receive significantly more email than if you were working in the office. The times when someone would stop by your office to ask a quick question are replaced with emails asking questions. Varying time zones and work hours can make a quick phone call unfeasible; these calls are often replaced with more emails.

> My colleagues and I are no longer able to simply see whether we're at our respective desks, and it can be easy to think that teammates are always available. I recommend that new managers utilize their out-of-office email auto-responses every weekend as soon as they step into their roles, so they can clarify from day one what their working hours are, how to best contact them, and when colleagues can expect to hear from them.
>
> In a role that necessitates quick responses, it can also be useful to take this one step further and set up an "away from my desk" message or a "delay in response" message any time you believe you'll take longer to reply to messages than normal. Technology has many ways to help us be visible the way that we want to be, and your auto-response can be one of them!
>
> —Christine Terrell

Scheduling specific times to check your email can be helpful. If you respond to an email each time one comes in, you will constantly be interrupted and have to shift focus. By turning email notifications off and only checking your inbox periodically, you will maintain focus on projects and complete them more efficiently. Many people benefit from checking email once in the morning and once in the afternoon. You may need to increase that number to three or four times a day, or you might need to check your email every hour. Over time, you will find what works best for you and is necessary for your role. When you do, manage the expectations of those you work with. Let your coworkers and clients know the best time to reach you by email.

If you are in a position that involves a significant amount of email, you may benefit from performing a sweep of your inbox when you start your workday. You can often use the sender and subject information to determine whether an email needs to be answered immediately. By taking care of emergencies first, you can move to the rest of your emails in a way that makes sense for you.

Some messages can be answered right away, while others require detailed responses that take more time. In general, if you can deal with an email in fewer than five minutes, you should answer or delegate it as soon as you open it; it is most efficient to read something once and take care of it immediately while you are thinking about it. For the emails that require more work than you can accomplish in five minutes, determine how much time you will need to properly answer. If you won't be able to compose an answer that day, it is best to send a quick response stating that you received the email and are working on it. If possible, include an estimated time frame for your full response. Then be sure to add that email to your to-do list.

Whatever the volume and urgency of the emails you receive, you should find a way to organize your emails properly. Different email systems have different tools to help with this. Find a simple way to denote emails that require further follow-up. Even though you should have added answering these messages to your to-do list, you still need an easy way to access the emails themselves later. Some email systems have a star function that lets you place a star next to emails to come back to. Other systems have different levels of importance that allow you to flag an email in various ways based on priority. Find a system that makes locating unanswered emails as easy as possible.

If, on the other hand, you have completed an email and no longer need it, many systems allow you to create folders to store old messages in. This can be a great way to clear out your inbox so that you don't feel bogged down. Become familiar with your email system and the features it provides so that you can use them effectively.

You may be in a position that requires you to be on email threads you do not actually need to read. For example, maybe you're a member of a cross-functional team that requires you to have a record of a certain type of transaction. In that case, you could benefit from applying email filters that automatically archive these messages and store them in a designated folder. If you use this system, it's a good idea to make sure the emails are still marked as "unread" so you know which ones you have seen before and which are new. You can then schedule a time once a day or even once a week to look at them. But be careful with this method: It can be common for people to completely forget about these folders and miss an important email that was filtered by mistake. Other people have found success using filters to automatically flag or label emails instead of archiving them. This has the benefit of helping you prioritize without the risk of missing the email altogether.

Another tool many people find helpful is nesting. This functionality automatically groups all replies and forwards of a particular message into one email thread. The benefit is a much clearer inbox: Each subject takes up just one line, and you can see all the responses in one place. This helps you to be sure you are seeing every response to the email chain before you chime in. However, some people find this method confusing, actually making it harder to read the entire chain and catch all of the pieces. This is particularly true if someone replies to everyone on the email and someone replies separately only to you, because both responses will be grouped into one chain. In any situation, it can be helpful to read the most current emails first to be sure you didn't miss a more recent response. Ultimately, the way you use the tools in your email client will be completely customized by you, for you. Try different things and see what works best!

Even with tools in place, the amount of time you need to set aside to answer emails will be very different depending on how many messages you typically receive in a day and how often you check them. Regardless, checking email does take time, so it is something you should schedule. To determine how much time to schedule for answering emails, start tracking how long it typically takes you to do so. Once you know how long it normally takes, you can allocate the proper time in your day.

Emails are a quick and effective method of communication. You can collaborate with multiple people at once, communicate outside of normal working hours, and have a written record of the conversation. Creating your ideal system for answering emails will ensure that you respond promptly and give those you work with a great impression of your ability and professionalism.

Chapter 4

Secrets of Communication

In a traditional office, if your colleague isn't responding to email, you can casually stroll past her office to see what's going on. The remote worker in Florida can't do the same with her colleague in Canada. In this section, we'll discuss how to get what you need while maintaining your professionalism.

Basic Etiquette

I used to work for a boss who was really accessible via Skype. It seemed like he was just always there, ready to answer any questions I had. Because of that convenience I really took advantage of it with all of my questions that came up in this new area that I was working in. One day, though, he made an offhand comment about how he organizes his day so that he can tackle most needs through email and then stay available for really time-sensitive concerns that people bring to his attention through Skype. I realized then that I was not choosing the right medium for all my questions and was taking up more of his time than I should have. I now make a strong effort to think about how I should reach out when I have questions to get what I need without slowing things down in the big picture.

—Mike Webber

In the virtual world, there are so many more ways to connect than you may be used to. Unlike the physical workspace, where you can pass someone in the hall, see them in their office, or take them out to lunch, there is a new horizon of virtual communication that allows you many different options for getting in touch. This new horizon comes with a caveat, though: Because your interactions with colleagues may now be fewer and farther between, it is more important than ever to be thoughtful in how you choose to communicate.

One obvious option is to send an email. In a traditional office, email may be reserved for longer communications, conversations with large groups, or exchanges that need to be documented. In the virtual world, all of these aspects hold true, but there is also more potential for quick emails back and forth that result in instantaneous communication. There are also many instant messaging applications. Your workplace may have one such platform or it may have several; it is important to become comfortable with each. Many instant messaging platforms allow you to set statuses or write updates for your coworkers to see—make sure you are using these features appropriately. There are other, more personal ways to connect as well, including voice calls and video calls.

Communicating in the remote workforce is a challenge since there is so much to consider. You need to figure out the right medium to communicate the right message in the right situation. For each message that you are trying to communicate, think about the preferences of the recipient. You may work with someone who hates email and would always rather set up a 15-minute chat. On the other hand, you may work with someone who loves how easy it is to manage email and prefers all communication be sent this way so that there is a record of it. Or, you may work with someone who is constantly in meetings but is able to answer instant messages throughout the day. When possible, communicate with people in the way that is best for them.

Which medium is best also depends on what you are trying to communicate. Some things are better said in a stored written format; an example would be communicating deadlines and deliverables to an entire team. Other content—for instance, sensitive information or difficult conversations—may be better handled over the phone. Often the best medium for conversations like this is a video call so that you and the other person can see each other's facial expressions.

If you have decided to communicate in a written format, remember that the written word creates a trail to follow. There is documented proof of everything you have said. It also forms a mental picture of you in the mind of your colleagues. In the virtual workspace, this may be all your colleagues use to get to know you. Thus, it is important to take the extra time to think about how your words will be translated over text. You may want to avoid slang and informal language so your words are not misinterpreted. It is a good idea to always stay as polite as possible and maintain proper grammar.

When drafting an email, there are many aspects to consider. One important area is the recipient field. Think about whom the email should be sent to. Also think about who should be copied. For example, if you are checking in on the status of a project that is due next week, it may not be appropriate to copy the main recipient's supervisor. Often, copying a supervisor can be seen as throwing someone under the bus or trying to get them in trouble in some way. However, if you are sending out a thank-you email to someone who finished a project ahead of schedule and did an excellent job, copying their supervisor is a great way to make sure that their accomplishment is recognized.

The subject line is an equally important aspect of email communication. The more informative it is, the better. Many companies have a protocol for emails that require special attention. You may be asked to write "Urgent" or "Please Respond" in front of subject lines that are time-sensitive or require a response. Alternatively, your team may choose to start the subject line with the project name and a colon so that everything regarding that project can be easily seen at a glance.

Be conscientious of email length. People you work with may save long emails for later, so be sure that your written word is succinct when possible. You may want to include bullets or numbered lists to highlight the points. Numbered lists are especially helpful when asking multiple questions because they allow the person to respond and answer by number. When you are responding to an email with multiple questions, it can be helpful to do so in another color so that it is easy to see the difference between the questions and their answers.

Throughout all communication, it is a good idea to be as clear as possible and make sure you understand what someone is conveying to you. Never assume that you know what the person means. If you have a question, ask it. Pay attention to the subtle unwritten and unspoken clues often present in communication; you ignore this subtext at your peril. There is a tendency to read written communication as more negative than what is meant. Before pressing send, read your message again to be sure it is conveying the intended tone. While communicating in the virtual world, there are many things to keep in mind. Being thoughtful in your communication choices will go a long way toward building understanding and good working relationships.

Setting Expectations and Achieving Transparency

One of the major differences between working in an office and working from home is your level of visibility. In an office or any other physical location where you are required to "punch in" (either formally or by virtue of being seen arriving on time), your absence can be quite conspicuous. When you are at meetings or visiting clients, a dark office or an empty chair at your cubicle clearly indicates that you're not present. If someone is looking for you, oftentimes the people who sit near you can tell your visitor that you are in another meeting. On your return, those same people can tell you who dropped by your desk.

Now consider the remote workforce. If colleagues and clients don't get email responses from you or are unable to see you online through various instant messaging programs, it could mean that you are in meetings or visiting clients. Or, it could mean that you are on an extended lunch break. Perhaps you're simply busy with projects and are ignoring communications from others for the time being. In a worst-case scenario, something tragic could have happened, and it could take a long time for anyone to realize you aren't around. Add different time zones into the mix, and you can see that setting expectations about your schedule and providing transparency about your whereabouts is an important part of succeeding in the remote workforce.

I start an ongoing conversation about expectations with my direct reports from our first meeting, premised on the idea that what I expect from them is what I should model for them. My reports—and my colleagues—can expect me to respond to their calls or emails within 24 hours during the week, but only for emergencies on weekends. They can also expect that I will value their time: I look at my calendar every morning, and when I notice that two meetings may overlap, I reach out to shift one of them proactively so that I can be fully present in every interaction. This gives me credibility when I address consistent lateness to meetings with my employees.

I am careful not to assume that my remote coworkers have the same availability I do. Just because I do something a certain way doesn't mean I have a right to expect it from someone else, so I learn whether colleagues are available on weekends before depending on them to help me with something urgent.

—Melody Young

The beauty of working from home is that in many cases, you have the opportunity to organize your own hours. That said, your coworkers should have a rough idea of your work schedule. Once you set your schedule, stick to those hours as much as possible so your colleagues and clients can plan accordingly. You could list your normal working hours in your email signature, on your web page, or in other locations where you have a digital work profile. When you will not be sticking to your regular schedule, use the out-of-office reply function to let those who email you know that they shouldn't expect an immediate reply.

Similarly, update your status in relevant messenger programs so colleagues and clients looking for you online know that you are not in the office. Instant messaging programs are very popular for colleagues to quickly and informally contact each other. Many of these programs allow you to display your status, showing whether you are online and available, offline, or online but unavailable. The challenge is remembering to update your status. For example, if your Skype status doesn't change for days, then it will soon become meaningless. Everyone will contact you at all times, because they assume that the "unavailable" setting is not actually true. The same goes for profile updates: If you don't maintain them, they too will lose their power. Make sure that you date your updates so that even if a message is left on display for too long, at least those reading it will be able to make appropriate assumptions about your true availability.

Setting expectations shouldn't be limited to your work schedule. Also make known how and when you will respond to people. There are some workers whose job duties, typing speed, or personal preferences allow them to reply to all emails and messages within 24 hours. However, there are those on the other end of the spectrum who cannot realistically respond to emails until certain days of the week or who much prefer to save responses for meetings. Either approach could work, but only as long as the people you interact with know what to expect. Many companies will have a formal or informal expectation regarding email response time, and that can be sufficient.

Instituting regular meetings can also help you to develop a high level of transparency and trust in those around you. This may not be an option for all remote workers, but where possible, having regular team and individual meetings can be another way to display your consistency. You can take this a step further. If you use a shared calendar program, those with access to your calendar will be able to see when your meetings are and identify patterns of when you are unavailable. Some programs also allow you to set your normal working hours on your calendar so others will receive a notification if they send you an invitation for a time outside of those hours. This can be particularly useful when dealing with people in different time zones who might want to talk with you during what is their morning, not realizing that you might not even be awake at that time.

As an employee in charge of your own schedule, you generally know what you'll be doing each day and what part of the day you'll be working. No one else will, however, unless you tell them. Help your coworkers by being transparent about when you are available and when you are not. Creating habits and patterns in the way you work allows others to learn what they can expect from you and when they can expect it. This builds trust, which is critical in the virtual environment where people can't see what others are doing.

Maintaining Professionalism

I follow the advice of Hall of Fame football player Deion Sanders: Look good, play good. Sure, I could get away with working in my pajamas all day, but I just don't feel like a professional when I'm not dressed as one. Instead, I wear clothes that put me in the right mindset and make me feel like I'm going to the office. This helps me do better work and signals to my teammates that I take their work seriously.

—Brian Sabel

The ability to choose whether to work in your office, in a local café, or just outside on your patio is a great part of working remotely. But the freedom to work anywhere comes with a new set of risks concerning the image that you project, as it can be very easy to skew overly casual in your attire and communication style. Most people don't start their remote workforce career wearing their pajamas on video calls or chatting to their colleagues in the same way as friends on social media, but professional standards can erode over time. If you have limited interactions with others, or if you have plenty of interactions but none with someone physically in front of you, it can be easy to unknowingly drift away from professional standards.

A remote worker donning traditional business wear on top, perhaps a suit jacket and tie, with a pair of casual shorts is an amusing picture to conjure up when thinking about the dress code of the virtual workforce. This fashion dichotomy most certainly happens, and naturally it's rarely an issue if it does, since remote workers are almost never seen from the waist down. One thing to consider is whether that lower-half comfort is coming at the expense of the work-home boundaries you've set for yourself. If you can maintain that distinction with only your top half being camera-ready, that of course is not a problem and is just another benefit of working from home. It is important to be aware, however, that there are times when you do need to stand up while on camera. You might need to grab headphones or deal with an interruption that requires you to leave the room. In those situations, if your lower half is not camera-ready, it could be awkward. Master the art of sliding out of camera view, or simply make sure you cover or turn off your camera before getting up. The safest option, naturally, is to be camera-ready from head to toe.

Casual Fridays have their place in the virtual world, though again this will depend on your boundaries, the people you need to interact with on camera, and your company's culture and expectations. It's a smart move to change your Skype status or other relevant indicators to prepare colleagues and clients for what to expect when you come on camera. They won't have the same visual cues as they would in a traditional office setting, where seeing employees in T-shirts and shorts quickly broadcasts the company dress code for the day. In a similar vein, be conscious that clanging jewelry, baseball caps, and loud shirts will not necessarily be camera-appropriate on any day, even if they are distinct from your regular wardrobe. You might have your "work" baseball cap on, but it's not likely to be the best wardrobe choice when conducting meetings. Consider what is appropriate for both your personal needs and what the company expects from you. Acquire an appropriate wardrobe and keep up with your laundry so that what you choose to wear signifies to both you and those you interact with that you are ready to work.

In addition to knowing when to dress professionally and when to dress casually, it's important to know when to be formal and when to be casual in your interactions. For many people, going online and chatting with others over instant messenger or in video calls is rooted in friendly and social interactions. When using those methods of communication in the work environment, it can be challenging to find the right level of formality, as the instinct is often to veer into the casual. Resist this instinct. In the online working environment, it is usually safer to err on the side of being overly formal than to come across as too casual.

Consider how your email and typed chat messages will be interpreted. Who will be reading them? What is this person's position compared to yours? How well do you know them? Is there room for misinterpretation? A wise remote employee carefully considers these questions before hitting the send button and generally saves jokes for calls. When it comes to regular group calls, it can be helpful to set up a list of guidelines at the beginning. Outlining the dress code, the level of formality, and any other relevant points ensure that everyone is on the same page. You may find that the group functions better in an informal mode, but it's better to find this out up front than to make assumptions and risk being surprised.

Are there times when casual is better? Of course. Some organizations will hold game nights online, have virtual happy hours, or allot time for those higher up to mingle and interact with subordinates. Outside of these structured events, talking one-on-one with colleagues you know well can provide you with the chance to relax and have a fun conversation. It's simply a matter of being aware of the people you're interacting with and recognizing that you're talking to colleagues and clients, not friends on social media.

"Be professional" seems like a strange thing to remind an employee to do, but those in the remote workforce should give themselves this healthy reminder from time to time. In an office setting, you receive immediate visual cues when you say something that borders on inappropriate, and you can make a mental note to phrase things differently next time. Clothing standards are reinforced every day when you see what your boss and colleagues are wearing. You can read the signals of your audience when speaking and make adjustments to your delivery in real time.

In the remote world, you often send information out into the ether and then have to read between the lines when you get a response. The opportunity to adjust on the fly is almost nonexistent. Even with video calls, it can be hard to read facial clues when there are image delays and audio glitches or when some participants are off camera. Just being aware of the situation, however, will allow you to maximize your chances of coming across in the way you intended. You can also be transparent about your attempts at finding the right level of professionalism and solicit feedback from your supervisor or colleagues. While it's important to develop your self-awareness, there's no reason why you can't get an outside perspective as well. You'll soon become an expert at projecting a professional air when it is required and a more casual one when the situation calls for it, so you can come across in exactly the way you intended.

Expressing Yourself

Think about a traditional office environment. Now picture the hardest worker in that office. Think of her as she works throughout a regular eight-hour day. This is someone who gets things done and doesn't allow herself to be easily distracted. She produces good work, which takes time, and she likely checks that work before sending it out. A good worker like her is probably too busy for small talk, so she keeps her conversations quick and to the point so she can get back to producing good, quality work.

> *I am retiring by nature, but I've found that I don't need to pretend to be an extrovert to work successfully in the virtual world. I have opened lines of communication by simply asking thoughtful questions. This can mean making it a point to speak up in large meetings, inquiring about changing business practices, or gathering input on a project I've been pouring myself into from colleagues with expertise beyond my own. Collecting feedback lets peers and higher-ups see my achievements, demonstrates that I am open to collaboration, and encourages others to feel invested in my efforts and growth.*
>
> *—Caitlin Duke*

Now picture this worker in the virtual workforce. But remember, you can't see her because she's working at home, so all your interactions are done online. This person may still be a good worker who produces quality work, but few people will know. This is one of the most interesting and, for some, most challenging parts of working virtually. Hard work that no one can see does not translate into success. It simply makes you a hard-working ghost.

In the remote workforce, you must demonstrate that you are a good worker by managing your persona in a conscious and deliberate manner. The long-standing practice of keeping your head down, doing great work, and being recognized for those efforts doesn't work in the virtual environment. You need to be more visible, even about mundane matters, because otherwise you are quite literally out of sight and therefore out of mind.

So what does this *not* mean? It doesn't mean changing your persona into something you are not. If you are someone who has always let your work speak for itself, you don't need to transform into a self-promoter who is constantly making big announcements about your progress. A transformation is necessary, but not one that radically changes who you are. Instead, you'll need to consider how to be a visible employee in terms of the choices you make in your interactions with colleagues. Consider it akin to dressing for success—only in this situation, you're showing your work accomplishments rather than your new tie.

This also doesn't mean that a great online presence makes up for poor work or poor productivity. Talking a good talk will mean little if the results aren't there to back it up. Virtual workers who lack the substance to support their presence are quickly identified. Indeed, with the greater trust placed between an employee and an employer in the remote workforce, a breach of that trust has greater repercussions. Be honest and be appropriate. Let those you work with know you're working and that you care about getting the job done.

Creating your persona and promoting yourself take effort. You are not visible unless you consciously take action. Your company will likely have different communication processes set up, which could include group instant messenger chats, virtual communities, email chains, and so on. Take the initiative to make good use of those forums to share what you're working on and create a fully realized picture of yourself in the minds of those in your workforce. For some people, this kind of interaction may not come easily, but with time, even quiet individuals can learn to comfortably share what they need to with their colleagues.

Interestingly, someone who is an introvert can actually thrive in this kind of environment. Many individuals who are fairly shy and not particularly adept at in-person social situations can become almost unrecognizably outgoing in their online interactions. Not just through typed communication but even on video calls, these people function quite well in situations where much of their social discomfort is filtered out through the curtain of technology. Thus, if you're concerned that you don't have the outgoing personality one thinks about when picturing a highly visible and chatty employee in the non-remote environment, rest easy. This new world could very well fit your personality in a way that an office workspace never would.

This doesn't mean that extroverts should avoid working remotely. The virtual workforce can expose you to groups of people whom you might not have otherwise met. You could have colleagues in different cities, different states, or even different parts of the world. Office banter, via instant message, can even be better, as introverted colleagues are more apt to join in the witty (written) repartee. While it may not be possible to meet after work for happy hour, many virtual employees have found that an online video happy hour can be just as fun.

Remember, the virtual work environment is an altogether different world, with different rules and parameters. Bringing out your online persona means making conscious decisions to connect with others. Forming your online persona means choosing what you say. You won't need to develop a new vocabulary per se, but rather a different way of expressing yourself. Online communication can be prone to misunderstandings, so using emoticons and keeping comments short and simple are all part of interacting effectively with colleagues. Modulating your message and tone will ensure you are seen as not just a good worker but also someone who is present and engaged with the whole team.

It's an exciting opportunity, working online. You get to craft your persona in a way not typically afforded by working in a traditional office. Naturally outgoing individuals can funnel that social personality into vibrant virtual connections. More introverted types have a chance to flourish and connect with a lot of people in an engaging way that allows them to remain comfortable. Regardless of where you fit on this spectrum, being visible is essential in the remote workforce. Do your work to be seen in a positive light, and you will set yourself up for even greater success down the road.

Working with Your Boss

It's important to know how often your boss wants to meet with you. My boss and I had a standing one-on-one appointment once a week that worked well for us. And then last year, as we were thinking of ways to become more agile, we decided to try meeting for 10 minutes every day instead. We phrased these daily meetings as a pilot, and had even set up the calendar invite so that it would end after a certain number of weeks.

Unfortunately, we didn't have the discipline to stick to a 10-minute slot. The 10-minute meetings quickly became 20-minute meetings, which turned into 60-minute daily meetings. We always had plenty of actual work tasks to talk about, and the conversations were good, but our schedules could not accommodate a standing 60-minute meeting. Once our pilot was over, we agreed to return to meeting once a week, with ad hoc communication as the need arose.

—Patrick Reagan

In business, if relationships aren't king, they are at the very least the power behind the throne. Nowhere is this truer than in the relationship you have with your boss. All bosses have the potential to be an advocate and also a gatekeeper. In the virtual workforce, your manager's influence over your brand is much more pronounced. Work hard to get this relationship right; you will be more engaged and effective in your role if the person you report to is your ally. For some companies and many supervisors, managing a virtual team is new territory. It's one thing to manage a single freelancer while working in a traditional office. It's quite another to manage an entire team of virtual workers while also working from home.

If your company is new to the remote workforce, your boss may be grappling with how to manage you effectively when she can't see you. Be persistent—and polite—when asking for what you need. Above all, go into this relationship assuming that the person you report to wants to help you succeed. If your boss doesn't answer your questions in one medium, try another. Do not mistake a lack of responsiveness for a lack of interest. They could be working at the task at hand and just not providing any updates. If you still don't get a response, try reaching out to a more veteran colleague to get the answers you need. If you do get an answer to your question from someone else, be sure to let your manager know. Your colleague in the same role may also lack resources, or he may not. A cross-functional colleague you work with every day may also have that information. You won't know until you ask. Word your requests as neutrally as possible and keep a virtual paper trail.

Conversely, many new virtual managers try to micromanage their way through the remote world. If your manager is micromanaging you, understand that this isn't necessarily about your manager's lack of trust in you; it may be a response to uncertainty. Luckily, there are things you can do to help your manager navigate this unfamiliar territory.

If you are unsure about any aspect of your job, ask! Err on the side of too much communication at the beginning, then gradually dial it down until you get to a communication level that works for both of you. This might mean living with micromanagement for a little while, then calling a meeting to discuss communication expectations now that you have both had a chance to get to know one another better.

We all have a preferred way to interact with our colleagues. Your manager is no different when it comes to interacting with her direct reports. Among other things, you want to figure out where she stands on the formal-informal spectrum. Does your boss like joking with her direct reports, or does she prefer to keep all communication centered firmly on the task at hand? Does she prefer meetings or written reports? While there may be some room for flexibility on these issues, you will get along better if you understand that you will need to adapt to her style more than she will adapt to yours.

Every role has performance metrics. Some companies may post scorecards for each role on the company intranet. Even if your company doesn't do this, you can often figure out what is most important to the person you report to by paying attention to what she asks for and when she asks for it. Ask questions. Make it clear that you want to ensure you give her exactly what she needs.

Ask for feedback. In a perfect world, you would receive thoughtful, balanced feedback about your performance on a regular basis. In the real world, day-to-day concerns can crowd out these larger conversations unless you ask for them. This is especially true in the virtual setting, where everyone works more and you are literally out of sight for most of the day. If, for whatever reason, you don't receive feedback on your performance, try to elicit it by asking specific questions. "How am I doing?" is not a specific question. "On a scale of 1 to 10, how well would you say I get along with others?" is better. If you change the way you do something in response to your boss's feedback, let her know. This sends the message that you value her opinion and want to do a good job.

In almost all cases, you will settle into a mutually productive working relationship. If this doesn't prove to be the case, then try to identify the problem. Diagnosing issues can be challenging in the remote workforce, where it is all too easy to feel isolated if things are not going well. Still, there are steps you can take to get the help you need.

Sometimes the problem between you and your manager centers around differences in working style. It is all too easy for this type of conflict to look like a performance problem. For example, if you are the type of person who needs to think about something ahead of time and your boss needs to talk things out in the moment, your boss may draw the wrong conclusions about your strategic thinking ability. How you handle this type of friction depends on the personalities involved.

In some cases, you can call a meeting and try to address the issue directly. You might do this by saying something along the lines of, "I've noticed that we've had some conflict, and I would love to find a way for us to both get what we need." In other cases, this is not possible. Your network can be a resource here as well. First, a trusted member of your network can act as a sanity check. Ideally, this person is well connected and has a good sense of the company culture and the wider goals of your unit. Are you being reasonable? It can be hard to hear that you are the problem, but if this is the case, then denial does not help you. If your boss is the problem, then your colleague may have ideas that can help you to either endure or change your situation.

There are also things you can do on your own. Make sure that you are doing an excellent job in your role. Do not let your performance metrics dip. This might also be a good time to excel on other projects for other departments. If you are seen as an asset by other members of your leadership team, it can mitigate your boss's perspective of you. You might even be able to use the managers of these other projects as references if you decide to look for a different internal role.

Many virtual employees have found that being managed remotely provides a great mix of immediate interaction and uninterrupted work time. In the vast majority of cases, applying a little patience and doing a little detective work will help you develop a great working relationship with your boss.

Working Effectively with Others

> *I learned the hard way that, especially in a remote workplace, face-to-face video calls promote relationship building better than email exchanges. Though I love writing emails—I can write them at times convenient to me, and I'm able to mull over my words and craft my messages carefully—they don't allow for the multi-dimensional variables that arise in a live conversation. Furthermore, if I find myself saying, "No, I don't want to call; I'll just write an email," I know that I need to examine why I don't want to speak to that person and improve that working relationship.*
>
> —Yeo Ju Choi

From the moment you start interacting with a new team, you should begin to form an idea of how the team operates. In a physical workspace, you can casually view the interactions of your coworkers just by being in the same space and observing them. In the virtual workplace, you can do the same thing, just in different ways.

Many teams use some sort of instant messaging app and may even have a group chat. If so, you can join the group chat and in the beginning simply observe how your coworkers interact with one another. From a group chat, you can determine how formal or informal a group is as well as the purpose of the chat. It might be a way for coworkers to engage in fun banter throughout the day to keep things interesting, or it may be a quick way to get questions answered. Knowing the purpose can help you determine how often to check the group chat and how to interact within it.

Your team may also have regularly scheduled virtual team meetings. Again, in the beginning this can be a great way to observe how team members interact with one another. You may find that the interactions in chats are the same as in group meetings, or you may find that the tone is very different. The differences may be due to who the participants are in each format, such as whether a direct supervisor or a member of senior management is present, or due to the format itself. Your team may use the group chat to joke around and the team meetings to get things accomplished, or vice versa. In the virtual workforce, it's not uncommon to have different dynamics on different platforms within the same team. You can facilitate your relationship with your team by understanding which communication medium is used for what.

Responsiveness and frequency of communication are also important. Your team may have standards as to how quickly you need to reply to emails, instant messages, and other forms of communication. When you know the standards, you can follow them. The same goes for following up with team members. If your team has a standard of a one-week response time, for instance, you wouldn't want to follow up after three days. However, if your team has a one-day response time, it would be appropriate to follow up after that time has passed.

You can apply this advice not only to working with your team but also to working with outside teams. If you are selected to work on a project with another group, or if you communicate with another team in general, you will want to pay special attention to how their team norms differ from those of your "home" team and adjust your approach accordingly. When in doubt, ask! If you are still uncertain about what is expected of you, let the outside team know how you will interact with them unless told otherwise. That way, there is no ambiguity about what you are going to do.

Knowing your role within the team itself can also have an impact on how you work with your coworkers. If you have been brought in as a leader, you should pay close attention to how the other leaders within the team act. If you were brought in to replace someone else, it could be helpful to gather information about how this team member worked with others, paying special attention to the things that they did well and learning from the things that didn't work as well.

Getting along with your coworkers in the virtual workforce doesn't have to be any more difficult than getting along with people in a traditional office. In some ways, it can be easier, as you don't have to listen to their choice of music or smell what they had for lunch. With a little patience and dedication, you will soon develop positive working relationships with the people you interact with to meet goals and produce results.

Managing Indirect Reports

When you're interacting with your direct reports, there is a clear understanding of your working relationship. You assign tasks, and your staff completes them. If something doesn't go according to plan, you can set expectations and provide immediate feedback. Guidance and disciplinary action can be applied when you feel they are needed. If you recognize someone on your team is ready to grow, you can directly craft their progress, getting them ready for additional opportunities.

Managing indirect reports isn't as straightforward. This is true whether you are in a traditional office setting or a remote one; the biggest difference between the two is the degree to which you need to actively build in communication points. In an office environment, you might regularly see an indirect report working away at various tasks. A casual glance from your vantage point across the room may tell you how she is progressing or if she needs you to intervene. You may have regular and close contact with your indirect report's boss, so updates can easily and often casually be shared. In the remote workforce, none of these visual cues are present. If you want to successfully manage your indirect report, you need to build in your own feedback loops.

Success in managing indirect reports often comes through developing a trusting relationship. It's best to start by trying to understand the needs and motivation of the indirect report.

Does this person want to be doing this work, or have they simply been assigned to fill a need? Is it a chance for them to prove they can do different work and participate on a new team in order to strengthen their internal resumé? Or are they struggling on their current team and potentially going to be transitioned elsewhere? Knowing their situation and any relevant backstory will help you assess how someone is feeling so you can act accordingly. While you don't need to know exactly where this indirect report is coming from in order to have a successful working relationship, having this information can go a long way in helping you understand the best way to work together. By doing the right level of research on who you're working with, you can then make sure you're both operating on the same page.

Piecing together your indirect report's backstory may seem complicated when you work remotely, but a little preparation and thought can help you get what you need. This could include learning how this individual already works with their boss, understanding any recent performance concerns or successes, or researching any other events (past or ongoing) that could impact how they respond to your management style. This person, regardless of whether they are an all-star or someone with performance issues, is going to be used to carrying out duties in a way that reflects the needs of the person whom they report to. You may have different, though equally effective, ways of working that don't mesh well with this person's habitual style, leading to frustration, mistakes, and inefficiency. Recognizing where your indirect report is coming from and then establishing clear expectations with them from the start is crucial. This is especially true in the remote workforce, where you won't necessarily know that something is wrong until a significant amount of time has passed or certain tasks are already completed.

It's also important to consider when and how to loop others in. Is it really necessary to copy your indirect report's boss on every email? Probably not, and aside from filling your colleague's inbox with unnecessary emails, it can also set up a relationship that is not based on trust. A better option is to have regular check-ins with your colleague to provide updates about how her direct report is doing while working for you. Sharing a version of those conversations with the indirect report also keeps things out in the open. This makes the process just formal enough and gives you the opportunity to present any concerns in a safe way with a trail of evidence. This can be especially important if you don't have a close relationship with the indirect report's boss or even if you don't know that person at all. That way, if there are concerns, they won't cause as many problems as they would if there were no warning at all.

You definitely want documentation about your experiences with an indirect report. With your direct reports, you get to know them well and you have a clearer picture in your head about how they are performing. You also don't need to communicate as much about them to others. In contrast, you need to be able to pass on updates to the managers of indirect reports whenever needed. If you don't have good examples of how they are doing, you won't come across very well. So keep notes on how they do and you'll not only be doing everyone else a favor, you'll be doing one for yourself as well.

—Mike Webber

You should feel comfortable providing feedback to your indirect report, but if it's feedback that has implications for his regular work, then that feedback should be given with his direct supervisor involved. This is a sensitive path to navigate, because it can sometimes be seen as getting an employee in trouble by looping in his boss. This is why having a strong foundation of clear communication and regular updates is important. Then, if there is an issue that needs to be raised, it's not going to be a surprise for anyone involved, and it's not going to stand out as more serious than it actually is. If you have already provided feedback to the employee about his performance and you don't feel formal communication with his boss is necessary, then a short, personal update to his boss might be sufficient instead. Human resource issues, however, will likely require the employee's direct manager to take the lead, even if the work is being done for you or your team.

Managing others who don't report to you can be a great experience. You get to meet new people, expand your network, and learn about different management and working styles. But of course the challenges of dealing with indirect reports need to be managed as well. Clear and regular communication with both the worker and their supervisor is key, and if your company doesn't have a system in place for this type of interaction, it will be up to you to create one. Find out what works for everyone involved and then provide a consistent communication experience. The remote workforce thrives on good systems of communication, and these systems are especially important when it comes to managing those who report to others.

Running Virtual Meetings

Test out your audiovisual setup with a trusted friend or colleague before hopping into a larger video call. Virtual meetings require some considerations that in-person meetings don't. For example, when I started my remote role, I often jumped into my team meeting without thinking about the camera angle. I was known as "Wilson" (from the show Home Improvement*) because my camera only showed half of my face!*

—Kristin Robinson

When first shifting from in-person meetings to virtual ones, it can seem that virtual meetings are less important or even that they don't really feel like meetings. However, in the virtual workforce, these meetings are often all you have. They are real meetings and should be treated as such.

In a virtual meeting, make sure everyone is heard. Some people feel more comfortable talking in person than electronically. If people are on camera, you can pay attention to physical cues. You may notice that someone wants to speak from their facial expression. If you are in an audio-only meeting, it can be helpful to have a list of attendees to reference. You can then go down the list, asking for each person's thoughts or updates.

There are also ways to make sure that everyone at a meeting is on a level playing field. For example, if three people are working remotely and three are in the office, it can put everyone on more even ground for the three in the office to stay at their desks on their personal computers rather than meet in a conference room together. Grouping some, but not all, people together can create an us-versus-them dynamic in the room. It can also make it easier for the on-site people to have side conversations, which can be distracting to the remote participants and cause people to miss information. By putting everyone in a similar situation, you can help to ensure that everyone feels included and equal.

Make your meeting time count. Some issues are better resolved with an email or a phone call than with a meeting. Additionally, it is best to have a limited number of topics to discuss in each meeting. For example, if you are working on five projects simultaneously with the same team member, it may be best to plan to talk about only a couple of those projects at each meeting. It can also be helpful to send out an agenda prior to some meetings. When everyone knows the planned topics ahead of time, everyone can be prepared, and meetings can adhere to the time frame (and topics) given.

Always prioritize your discussion topics so that you hit the important points before the meeting is over. When there are 5 to

10 minutes left in the meeting, determine whether the remaining items on your list can be covered in that time or if another meeting should be set up. It is often better to schedule an additional meeting than to rush through important topics or potentially cause the meeting to run over. Ending a meeting on time is best for everyone involved.

However, meetings do not always stick to the scheduled time. In the physical workspace, it can be easier to end a meeting on time because you have tangible restrictions, such as other people needing the meeting room. Or there may be physical cues that it is time to end, such as people fidgeting or looking at the clock. In the virtual world, the lines become more blurry. Hopping from one virtual meeting to the next is as simple as clicking a few buttons. However, it is equally important to end meetings on time in the virtual workspace, because allowing yourself to be lax can often lead to being a couple of minutes late to the next meeting without even realizing it. Treating every meeting as though there is a hard stop at the end of it is the best way to be respectful of people's time and ensure a smooth workday.

There are ways to help meetings end on time. If you are the meeting organizer, plan content that will fit in the time allotted. When working remotely, you can't steal a few minutes in the break room or the hallway to quickly catch up with colleagues. Thus, these quick catch-up conversations usually happen during meetings. Plan a few minutes at the beginning and the end of the meeting as a buffer. For example, if the meeting is set for an hour, you can plan 45 minutes of content. This extra time leaves room for catching up, questions, late arrivals, and technical difficulties. Some calendar programs allow you to set shorter run times for appointments—25 minutes instead of 30, or 50 minutes instead of an hour—which builds in a bit of a buffer for team members to take a break or mentally prepare for the next meeting. However, meeting participants will only benefit from these buffers if you adhere to scheduled end times.

Sometimes running late for a meeting is inevitable. When you are going to be late for a meeting in person, often the other person you are meeting can physically see that you are not at your desk. They may even be able to see that you are in another meeting simply by looking through the window of a conference room. In the virtual world, this is not possible. When someone enters a virtual meeting space and you are not there, that person often has very little recourse to find out where you are or what is keeping you. If you are running late for a meeting, send a quick message to the person you are meeting to let them know your estimated time of arrival. This can be short and to the point: "Stuck in meeting— will be 10 min late" is sufficient. If there are other people in the meeting, they may decide to start without you since you will be 10 minutes late, whereas they might have chosen to wait for you if you were only a couple of minutes behind. If you are late to a meeting with only one other person, that person can use the extra 10 minutes to answer a quick email or grab a bite to eat. Keeping others informed shows that you respect their time.

One way to ensure you are on time for meetings is to schedule a true break between the meetings themselves. If you have a meeting from 2:00 p.m. to 3:00 p.m., don't schedule the next one until 3:30 p.m. A half-hour buffer is perfect to account for a meeting running a couple of minutes late. Actually scheduling these buffers into your calendar is a great way to ensure nothing else will be scheduled during those times. Another benefit of scheduled buffers is that they allow you to debrief. Some meetings have takeaways and action items for you to perform. Giving yourself a few scheduled minutes to document your new tasks (or perhaps even accomplish a couple of them) can give you a firm handle on your day.

Virtual meetings can be a great tool for getting a lot of work done in a short period of time. By properly planning all aspects of your virtual meetings, you will find that life in the remote workforce is more productive and more enjoyable—for you and for your colleagues.

Communicating Urgency and Need—and Following Up

Your work doesn't exist in a vacuum: At some point over the course of your workweek, you'll need something from someone, or someone will need something from you. Sometimes the request is easy and your colleagues are willing to help you. Other times, people are busy and resources limited. Communicating the level of urgency of the thing you need—and getting what you need in return—is an art unto itself.

We've all encountered that colleague (let's call him Frantic Frank) who needs everything *right now*. Perhaps you have even dropped everything to help Frantic Frank get something done, only to find out that the "emergency" was all in his mind. Or maybe you've run into his polar opposite, Silent Sally. Silent Sally doesn't tell you that she is overwhelmed or unable to complete a task until her deadline passes, and her lack of communication means you miss your deadline, too. The Frantic Franks and Silent Sallys of the remote workforce soon develop a reputation as untrustworthy or hard to work with.

To be successful in any career, you should do your best to avoid becoming Frantic Frank or Silent Sally and, instead, identify and manage your interactions with these types of colleagues. This requires more than knowing how to do your job. First, you must understand what you need. Most needs fall into one of four categories (information, access, skills, or authorization), and the category of need determines the level of legwork you can do ahead of time. If you need someone to authorize your budget, for example, you can often collate all the relevant data in an easy-to-digest email or spreadsheet so the authorizing person can simply glance at the information and make a decision. If you need information, you can research whether the information is already housed somewhere else before you reach out to a colleague. Once you've done your due diligence, you can feel good about asking for what you need. Your manager, or a more veteran colleague, can often help you determine which department handles the type of request you have and which person in that department can help you. Asking the right person for help is key to actually getting the help you need.

Once you know what you need and who can assist you, you can think about when to approach that person for help. In a traditional office setting, you can swing by someone's desk and, if she doesn't look busy, ask for a minute of her time. In the remote workforce, you can't see people, and you will often have dozens of colleagues in different departments across multiple time zones. In these circumstances, it's vital to develop a sense of your target's work rhythm. Is this person busy with payroll on a certain day? Does she reserve mornings for time-sensitive work? Is she out on the road making sales at the end of the month? You might have better results if you wait for a time that is more convenient for her.

Now that you know when to approach your colleague, you can think about how to approach her. This step is especially important if the person is in high demand. You want to make your request as attractive and as easy to answer as possible. This starts with clearly and succinctly stating your need, followed by briefly detailing the steps you have taken to try to resolve the task on your own. Make sure to include a time estimate as well. Something like, "Hey Mary, can you confirm that sales are up 3 percent this year? Joe said I have to get that info from you. I'm presenting our results to our department next week," is much more effective than an email that simply says, "Do you have a second? I want to pick your brain."

Communicating what you need and when you need it helps everyone prioritize the work that needs to get done. In the remote workforce, you can't see what people are working on. You can't tell if someone is overwhelmed, or needs more training, or was just handed a project that takes precedence over yours. Because of this, you need to set a follow-up schedule that matches the importance and urgency of the the project at hand. If the task is simple and non-urgent, or your company has guidelines for how long it should take to complete certain tasks, then you might wait until the due date to check in. If the task has many moving pieces, is ambiguous, or has a hard deadline, then you may want to set up multiple check-in points.

If I need something from somebody, that is the first thing I say, right in the subject line of my email—what it is and when I need it. In the body of the email, I also make sure they understand why I'm asking for it. This leaves no doubt about what I'm talking about.

For my direct reports, I use a formula in the subject line: Action Required: (whatever the ask is) and Due Date: (deadline). For people who don't report to me, I omit the "Action Required" and "Due Date," but still state what I need and when I need it. I have also learned that people's communication styles are different, so it is crucial to find out how people work and reach out accordingly. Some members of my team like me to tell them what I need and then to get out of the way. If what they produce isn't good enough, then we can have a discussion on how to fix it for the future. Other members of my team come to me several times during the course of the task because they need to talk it out.

But even in time-sensitive situations, I try to avoid being so solutions-oriented that I bulldoze over my team. It can be hard in the moment, when everything is coming at you from seven different directions, to pull back and let someone else handle the issue. You have to be open to the idea that they may do a better job of solving the issue, and you will be the one to change your approach the next time that same issue comes up.

—Bobby Amirebrahimi

This is true whether you are managing the entire project or only one piece of it. As a project manager, the list of things you need to keep track of can seem endless, but the general categories of those things tend to fall into one of four areas: access, information, skill, or bandwidth. Some of the questions to ask yourself include the following: Are things progressing on schedule? Does anyone look or act stressed or overwhelmed? Does everyone have what they need to do the job? Does everyone understand what to do? Conversely, if you're an individual contributor on a project and the project manager hasn't set up check-in points, set up your own check-in schedule. You want to make sure you are doing the work expected of you in the time frame required, and it's far easier to salvage a situation if you catch a problem early. If the project changes scope or you are handed a new, higher-priority project, then you need to discuss and adjust timelines and expectations as soon as possible. As a project manager, you can't assume that the colleague who agreed to spend five hours working on your project can stay on for another 20. Similarly, as a member of a project team, you must communicate proactively if your bandwidth changes.

In a perfect world, your colleagues stay in regular communication with you as you work together on projects. Unfortunately, sometimes your colleagues become unresponsive and you have to loop in others. It is important to remain professional and give people the benefit of the doubt when doing so. Keep your tone understanding and make it clear that you are looking for the best way to proceed, instead of throwing someone under the bus. Whether the person is on your team or a different team, your supervisor is often the best person to reach out to first. Your supervisor may be able to follow up with the person directly or point you in the right direction in terms of who you should follow up with next. When possible, follow your company's appropriate chain of command and established guidelines for whom to contact and when.

Communicating urgency and need in a way that builds trust and doesn't paint you as a Frantic Frank or a Silent Sally takes some thought. If you consistently work at it, you will soon be known as someone who is dependable and a pleasure to work with.

Venting Appropriately

> *Many years ago when I worked for a different company, I spoke to a colleague about how handy I found Skype to be, where I could just Ctrl-F to find information shared by others in our chats. She let me know that wasn't an option for her because she cleared her history at the end of each day, because she spent a lot of time venting there and she didn't want anyone to see it. It was an eye-opening conversation, because up to that point I hadn't thought about filtering the things I type in chat. I never said anything unprofessional, but what you type lasts a long time unless you take steps to clear it.*
>
> —Mike Webber

Even if you love your job and are genuinely excited to begin each day, there can still be parts of your work that frustrate you. It could be problems with a coworker, difficulties with administrative processes, or sudden changes to deadlines and tasks that result in your having to cancel or change personal plans. While taking deep breaths, counting to 10, or getting outside for a vigorous walk around the neighborhood are all effective ways to deal with stressful work situations, venting is another effective technique. However, figuring out the appropriate way to vent in the remote workforce is quite important.

It is crucial to choose carefully the audience for your venting. Ideally, you should have the type of open relationship with your boss that allows you to vent without penalty. This individual is responsible for your development and most likely, in the remote workforce, knows you better than anyone else. It can be easy to assume that you have a close enough relationship with someone else to freely vent about a frustrating situation, but do you? Are your few instant messenger chats with a colleague enough for you to take the further step of complaining about a part of your job that is frustrating you? It's easy to have many short interactions with someone online and feel like you know them reasonably well, but be careful. Consider your position and that of the person you want to vent to. If this person is a subordinate, hearing you express frustration about your job may cross the line into inappropriate territory a lot sooner than if the situation were reversed. While it's important that those who report to you (directly or indirectly) get an accurate view of the work you do, there may be a larger amount of sensitive information you could end up sharing that may color the perspective of the other person in large ways. Keep your venting to those you have regular, in-depth interactions with because they have a broader context for the negative emotions you're expressing. Venting to someone you don't know that well could negatively affect the way they think of you or the organization as a whole.

The medium you choose for venting is also important. A video call may be best, because you can see the other person's reactions better and adjust as needed. You're less likely to cross the line by saying something inappropriate for the workplace when you are actually looking at another person and not just staring at your wall while on the phone. Even riskier is venting via typing. You should avoid putting your frustrations down in a recordable format like email or digital chat. Something in writing has the potential to not only last forever but also be retransmitted to an unintended audience and be easily misinterpreted.

You'll also need to choose the appropriate time to meet with someone to vent. When you're working in an office, it's easy to see when your colleague or boss looks free. Even more conveniently, there are many opportunities to take coffee breaks together or do a shared lunch. In the online environment, especially when dealing with different time zones, you need to pick and choose your moments appropriately. Can you easily take 10 minutes of a call with a boss or coworker to vent and then resume your regular agenda? Is asking someone for a few minutes of their time a part of your company's culture, or does doing so signal that you have something serious to say? Pick and choose these moments carefully so you don't make the venting process seem more formal than it is. Remember also to make these *moments*, not extended periods. Regardless of the situation, venting for over an hour is likely inappropriate no matter the topic or audience.

Finally, you need to consider the proper way to frame venting. In most cases, it's best to let your listener know that you need a few minutes to let off some steam about an issue that is troubling you. The virtual workforce is full of lasting first impressions, so if this is the first time you're venting, you will want to make sure you're doing so in a way that shows you can see the bigger picture and are venting for stress relief, not to just complain for the sake of complaining. This is especially important when venting to your boss but can also be a valuable consideration when dealing with colleagues who may not know you that well outside of regular workplace interactions. You should also be conscious of your word choice and tone when expressing your frustration. A vent session is not a free-for-all but rather a controlled way of expressing your frustration so that you don't let it build up, resulting in higher stress and perhaps the desire to quit. Venting can also lead to productive solutions. A savvy boss will use the opportunity to brainstorm resolutions or turn the experience into a teachable moment once the initial release of emotion has occurred.

It might sound like a lot of work to consider how to vent, which, after all, is an emotionally charged action that wants to be spontaneous. But that is exactly the point. Venting at work has its place, and it should be done in a controlled manner for you to glean its value without experiencing any of its drawbacks. You need the opportunity to vent to your colleagues, because who else will understand the troubles you are experiencing as you work in your remote office? But unlike in a traditional office, you can't hang up the phone after a frustrating conversation, sigh and rub your temples, and have a nearby coworker notice and offer up a sympathetic ear. As with most things in the remote workforce, you need to take charge of the situation to ensure that your venting remains a productive experience.

Chapter 5

Secrets of Professional Development and Growth

There are ways to remain visible and grow your career as a remote worker. This section will show you how.

Your Network

Even though a virtual network can have distinct differences from a physical one, there are many similarities, and a virtual network is equally (if not more) important to build. While the remote workforce gives you a unique ability to connect with many people in your organization, it's up to you to do so effectively and frequently.

Effective networkers are organized. Develop a framework that will allow you to make networking a regular part of your week. If you're new to the company, find out how your role fits within the overall business. An organization chart can be a helpful tool to picture how your company delivers its product or service. If your company doesn't have an org chart, ask questions until you can build your own. This will help you not only envision your future career path but also understand how different processes and people in the company interact with each other.

Create a list of people to speak to. This can be as simple as writing down the names and contact information of the people you will interact with the most or as detailed as a spreadsheet, ranking people in order of their importance to your work. You can also take the list a step further: Break it into categories to help you remember whom to contact for different situations. For example, you may have a list of leadership mentors you look up to and whose advice you value. And you may have a list of people you simply enjoy communicating with and want to keep in touch with on a professional level. Whatever segments you break your list into, the ability to easily contact someone when you need to is beneficial.

Once you have your list, schedule a 15- to 30-minute video call to get to know your coworkers. Most people enjoy talking about themselves. Ask your colleagues about what they do, what their pain points are, what they love about their job, and how you can best work together.

Take notes after each conversation. Don't rely on your memory to capture everything. Your notes should include a mix of the personal and professional and should grow over time. Knowing your colleagues' birthdays or favorite hobbies is just as important as knowing their skill sets. Staying active in virtual social circles can also help with this.

If you interact with someone on a daily or weekly basis, it can be helpful to schedule a regular call at a mutually agreeable time. For other colleagues, less frequent check-ins may be more appropriate, and these may be a casual email rather than a phone or video call. Schedule these into your calendar to make it more likely that you will actually keep your connections alive. Ask how things are going. Ask about that project they were working on (which you will remember because you wrote it down). Ask what they are working on next. If you do this regularly, you will soon have the opportunity to be of service to your colleagues. One colleague may mention that she wishes she could be more involved with training and development, while another colleague may say he wishes he knew someone who could help with the latest training project. Connecting these two colleagues makes you a valuable part of each person's network. Communicating regularly with the people in your network ensures you are not forgotten or lost in the shuffle.

It is also good to remember that a network isn't a static thing. Periodically reviewing your connections helps ensure that you communicate with each person at intervals that make sense. Take time to assess whom you want to communicate with more frequently and whom you'd like to communicate with less.

Your network is also your safety net. Know whom you can turn to if you need help. Different aspects of your job can require different types of assistance. Some colleagues can help you locate the right person to push a stalled project along. Others can help you navigate tricky interpersonal dynamics. Don't be afraid to ask for help. You will be far more efficient and effective if you do so.

I have two or three informal video calls scheduled per month with coworkers who have become friends. We talk about work, but we can also chat about anything on our minds. It is engaging for both parties and helps keep ideas flowing freely. I know it is time well spent, but even more important, our leadership sees value in us connecting virtually because we are physically separated. Unlike coworkers who share office space, we have to make these touch points happen purposefully to learn from each other.

—*Julie Minnich*

The remote workforce can connect you to people who are within your workplace yet far away geographically. This is a priceless opportunity to gain a different perspective on your business. At the same time, you may have to work harder at maintaining relationships because you will not physically run into people. Conduct your interactions with intention and frequency so that you can grow and maintain your network.

When you aren't limited by your geographic location, you can sometimes more effectively collaborate with people outside your immediate team. Master the art of the casual outreach. If you're working on a project, use that as an excuse to reach out to a stakeholder in a different department to gain his or her perspective. If you ever have an issue arise that you are unsure how to handle on your own, ask a more experienced colleague. Don't overlook more informal ways to connect with people. Talking about a shared love of sports, hobbies, or television shows are all acceptable ways to start a relationship with someone outside your immediate team. Take advantage of these different perspectives to learn new methods and strategies. You can also use your knowledge to contribute to parts of the company you may never have had access to otherwise.

You may find yourself interacting with people who hold a position in the company that is higher than yours but not in your direct line of command. While it's always advisable to maintain a level of professionalism and respect when dealing with others, this can be especially true when connecting with people in higher positions. Avoid complaining about various aspects of your job; instead, focus on positivity and solutions. Showing your best work and ideas to people in higher levels can help increase your visibility and open up new opportunities. Be strategic when taking on new opportunities. Always make sure your manager is informed of and on board with any outside assignments handed to you.

Starting on day one, invest the time to thoroughly understand and cultivate your network. As the weeks and months go on, continue to invest in maintaining and staying active in that network. Doing so will help you in your day-to-day activities and any future career path you choose to follow.

Recognition

Gaining recognition for your work yields many benefits, whether you wish to stay in your role or get promoted. You are seen as valuable and trustworthy. You may be given interesting assignments. Valuable people tend to be given more flexibility and autonomy. This can develop into a positive feedback loop, where you are increasingly seen as more valuable by working on the things that most interest you; this helps to build your reputation within your team and the greater company at large. This recognition is even more important in the remote workforce, where you are the sum total of your virtual interactions.

If you are someone who wishes to be recognized for your achievements, be the type of person who recognizes others. Be generous with your recognition. If a colleague helps you out, thank her in an email—and copy her boss. If a teammate spent extra time making your slides look good, make sure to mention that in a public setting. What goes around comes around. The people you recognize today may be the very ones who put in a good word for you tomorrow.

> *The company I worked for was going through some restructuring and I definitely wanted to make the cut, as other people I knew with more experience than I had were being laid off. I wound up with two different managers over that time period and both gave me advice on developing my brand, something I had never considered before. One suggested I become known as the manager who gets good results but that was quite broad and seemed like a high bar to clear given the state of the markets I inherited. The other boss suggested I specialize and, as one of the few managers with non-American markets, to make myself the reigning expert on all that was foreign. I dug in and years later, after I had moved into American markets, colleagues would still reach out to me with questions about best practices across the border.*
>
> —Mike Webber

But how do you gain recognition in the remote workforce? While there are many different actions you can take, the basic process is this: First, perform well. Then, promote yourself. Finally, cultivate recognition for your contributions. In the virtual world, it's your responsibility to promote yourself. Don't assume that anyone else is going to do this for you. Perhaps you are the type of person who cringes at the thought of promoting yourself. Fortunately, self-promotion doesn't have to be pretentious or insincere to be effective. Self-promotion simply means making sure other people know about your abilities and accomplishments.

Develop an authentic self-promotion strategy by first asking yourself a couple of questions: Who are you when you are at work? What do you stand for? Your answers develop the basis for your professional brand. Your brand can consist of your attitude, your work ethic, and your skill set, among other things. In person, your brand is naturally communicated through your words, your actions, and your physical presence. In the remote workforce, you must approach your brand more intentionally.

Build your brand around your strengths and personality. Are you someone who values harmony? Then in terms of attitude, you may brand yourself as being consistently positive and focused on solutions. Do you enjoy meeting people and building networks? Then you may decide to build your brand on this skill set, becoming known for being able to help colleagues connect with the right people to get things done. Are you someone who can't leave work until your inbox is cleared out? Then consider building your brand on your work ethic: be seen as the person who will finish a project on time, no matter what.

Make sure that your communication and work reflect your brand. Since you often won't be able to count on vocal inflection or physical expression to communicate your ideas, your written communication should always be drafted with your brand in mind. If you would like to be seen as someone who thoroughly plans out and crafts a response to each query, then make sure you do so. On the other hand, if you would like to be seen as someone who answers emails quickly, then do that. Be consistent in communicating your workplace brand, because consistency breeds trust.

Once you've settled on your brand, it's time to deploy it. As a remote worker, you are likely a member of various group chats or internal company message boards. These are natural places to organically promote yourself by publicly helping people solve problems. For example, let's say you decide to build a brand around your work ethic. If someone mentions in a team chat that they wish the company would provide a certain resource, volunteer to create it. Then share it with the group and send a copy of what you created to your boss. This is self-promotion through service, and it is highly effective.

This leads us into how to make your voice heard so you are visible within your organization. For you to be heard, others must consider you someone worth listening to. Notice that this is different from simply being vocal. First you demonstrate your expertise by performing well in your role and building value for the team. Then, when you communicate, people will want to listen. Of course, you must consider whom you should communicate with, what channel you should use, and whether the communication should be public or private. As you become more visible, your judgment will be valued just as much as your performance in your role. It may be that the best way to get your voice heard is to join a committee or task force. Working on cross-functional committees or projects is also a great way to get to know people outside your immediate team and disseminate your brand. Let your boss and colleagues know that you are available to help with these.

It is possible to cultivate visibility within the remote workforce. Spend time creating an authentic brand. Be on the lookout for opportunities to help solve problems. Over time, you will develop your brand and become known as a valued employee.

Soliciting Feedback

When you think of feedback, official performance reviews may come to mind. These reviews may affect things such as your future career path and salary. However, there are many other forms of feedback in the workplace. Each time you give a presentation, lead a meeting, or complete a project is an opportunity to collect information on your performance. In the physical world, someone may stop by your desk to let you know their thoughts. In the virtual world, you need to actively seek out that same feedback.

When you present in an important meeting, take note of the people in the virtual room. You can reach out to them afterward to gain their insight. When doing so, be targeted with your questions. In person, it can be easy to ask questions such as "How did it go?" or "What did you think?" and then build the conversation from there. However, these types of open-ended questions can be difficult to answer in the concise way required by virtual communication. Thus, you may not get the feedback you were looking for, or any response at all. Instead, be specific. If you tried out something new, such as using the pen function to write on a slide you were presenting, you can ask about that. If you waited five extra minutes before starting the meeting because you were missing a handful of people, you can ask the people who were on time how they felt about that. Any decision you made while presenting can be an opportunity to gain feedback. One way to collect this detailed feedback is to send out anonymous surveys afterward. If you choose to send out an anonymous survey, let your attendees know one is coming. Surveys are a great way for people to give you their honest thoughts without being concerned about consequences. Surveys also allow people to fill out their opinions on their own schedule.

> *Make giving and receiving feedback an expectation with your colleagues. When conducting performance reviews, my team's rule of thumb is that the outcome should never be a surprise, because we should be extolling excellent performance or supporting improvements consistently. In my last round of reviews, I tried something new suggested by a coworker: I asked each of my direct reports what feedback they had for me. Some were surprised and didn't have much to say, but others gave me specifics about communication and resources. I've had fantastic ideas come from just leaving these lines open, and I plan to continue this practice so that feedback becomes a natural part of all my conversations.*
>
> —Caitlin Duke

Of course, there will be times when you want a detailed breakdown from specific people on an entire presentation or project. The best way to gather comprehensive feedback is to do so live. Set up a virtual meeting with the person whose feedback you desire. Be respectful of that person's schedule and bandwidth.

Calling someone out of the blue to ask them to comment on every aspect of your performance on a project, for example, will likely not be as effective as setting something up in advance. Ask the person whether they are willing to sit down with you and give you their feedback. As with any other meeting, make the intention of the meeting clear. You will get more helpful feedback when you give people the opportunity to properly formulate their thoughts.

Make it easy for people to give you their honest opinion by preparing yourself to receive it. It can be easy to begin justifying your actions when someone gives you constructive criticism. Instead, take the time to thank them and write their words down to think on later. Accepting feedback in a positive way will build a positive relationship, often leading the person you consult to give you more and better information over time.

Garnering feedback can go beyond your boss, coworkers, and meeting attendees. It can be very helpful to learn what upper management thinks of your performance and why. Learning the opinion of those in higher positions can help you find areas of opportunity to work on and may even lead to resources to increase these skills.

Based on information gathered from others or on self-reflection, you may find that there are specific areas of opportunity you want to work on. Discuss with your manager the best way to learn and improve. Your company may have training videos to cover specific skills, or people in the company may possess the knowledge you're seeking and be happy to share it. Once you learn a new skill, test it out. If you learned a new scheduling technique, such as always scheduling meetings to end after 50 minutes instead of an hour, determine whether the new skill is beneficial and being used properly. You'll often get a sense on your own of how well something new worked, but this is also another great opportunity to ask for feedback.

The process of obtaining feedback never ends. No one is perfect, and there is always more to learn. Practice soliciting feedback; add it into your routine. When working remotely, there are still many ways to obtain the feedback and learning you desire—you just have to be more proactive about it.

Advancing Your Career

> *I was interested in moving forward with my career and tried a few different approaches to find a new role. I made some time to help out in a small way with a section of the company I was interested in exploring. They had me do some tasks with limited scope, and I enjoyed it and didn't break anything. Then a bigger project came up on the same team and they asked for me to come back and help in a larger capacity. I wouldn't have been asked to work on the bigger project if I hadn't volunteered my time on the smaller tasks. After having success there, when a spot opened up on the team, the manager approached me about the role and I was offered the job on the spot.*
>
> —Mike Webber

To grow your career in the remote workforce, you need to consistently keep your eyes and ears open. Be alert for any new opportunities, and be aware of the types of roles you would like to pursue in the future. In many workplaces these days, there are several different paths to career advancement. The road isn't always straight up; sometimes horizontal moves make sense for your professional development and skill set. In the virtual world, you don't have the ability to simply walk by someone's office, read their nameplate, and know their position. People won't pass you in the halls, eliminating the opportunity for other coworkers to tell you who that person is. However, paying attention to all the interactions you have can yield a rich array of information. Treat email signatures like nameplates; read them to find out the position and department of each person who contacts you. From there, you can gain insight into the roles and responsibilities of different positions. By understanding the myriad roles within the company, you can start to familiarize yourself with various teams and think about how you see yourself advancing in the future.

In meetings, pay close attention to the people in attendance and their positions. Their involvement in the meeting can indicate their relationship to the project and with the department as a whole. Matching those aspects with their job title can help you better understand the various responsibilities different positions hold. This information can help you determine how you would like to plan out your next steps. You may also learn about new skill sets you'd like to acquire or new projects you'd like to work on.

One way to get a feel for a role is to shadow someone. Shadowing is when you act as a bystander and observe how someone else completes a task. While this can be a great way to improve in your current role, it is also a great way to test out a potential role. In the remote workforce, shadowing works well if you can share screens and talk through particular tasks.

If you don't know where your company posts available positions, find out. Even if you are completely content in your current role, keeping an eye on current internal opportunities can expose you to positions you may never have been aware of before. You may find out about entire departments that you didn't even know existed. Periodically checking the virtual job board is also a good way to keep track of your coworkers and their progression. Being aware of how others move throughout the company can show potential paths available to you. As you browse job postings, be aware of the requirements of certain roles. Some roles may require you to live in a certain location or work a certain number of hours a week. Before you build a career path for yourself, make sure you understand the expectations of that path.

Taking on additional duties outside of your role can be another way to advance your career and gain visibility. When doing this, it's important not to spread yourself too thin. While visibility is important, the people you work with will be more inclined to recommend you for new things in the future if they see you succeeding at your main responsibilities.

Discussing your wants and needs in relation to your work responsibilities can have a positive effect on your career growth. The position you would like to move into may not be available right now, or you may apply for an opening but not be selected. Even in such cases, however, you have alerted people to the type of position you are interested in moving into. This can expand your visibility to other departments of the company that may not have interacted with you before.

If you do find a new job opportunity that speaks to you, speak up. Don't assume that someone will reach out to you or that your supervisor will contact you to let you know. It is your responsibility to let it be known that you want the new position. In most scenarios, you will want to talk to your immediate supervisor first before planning to apply to any new roles. This allows you to discuss with your supervisor your motivations for applying for the role and to be transparent.

Most importantly, consistently discuss with your supervisor the aspects of your job that you enjoy and any new aspects you are interested in. This can affect the assignments your supervisor gives you, which can improve your career path even within your current role. In some cases, this job crafting can lead to a completely different role created just for you. By continuously adjusting your current role to include more of the activities and projects you are interested in working on, you can slowly transform your current role into something more in line with your interests and goals, creating new directions for your career.

In both the traditional and virtual workplaces, you are responsible for your career and personal growth. In the virtual world, it can take more research to discover all the facets of your company and available opportunities for growth, but learning what you need to know is still doable. In fact, it is necessary for you to take charge of your career path and shape it to be exactly what you want.

Chapter 6

Secrets for Special Circumstances

The majority of this book deals with issues and opportunities that are true for most remote workers, regardless of the configuration of the team. This section will discuss some of the more common *uncommon* situations some may find themselves in.

Meeting in Person

> *Even though we chat nearly every day, it can still be intimidating to meet a colleague from the remote workforce in real life—we've never eaten lunch together or even sat next to each other.*
>
> *On the whole, though, I consider my relationships with my remote colleagues to be stronger than the relationships I've had with in-person colleagues precisely because we don't have physical proximity built in. We are forced to make that extra effort to go beyond the surface, effort that we wouldn't expend if we saw each other every day around the office.*
>
> *I have made it my mission to meet every person on my team in the flesh. I've found that I fall right in step with my virtual colleagues because we have spent so much time building the foundations of our relationships through our daily team chat. We know all the facets of each other's lives, so it's natural to call these colleagues my friends. Meeting them in person just makes them friends with legs!*
>
> —Chrissy Damasco

Remote employees can build strong working relationships with colleagues they never see in person. This is fortunate, as many remote workers will only ever connect through email, video, and instant messaging programs. There are others, though, who occasionally get to see their colleagues in person. If you have such an opportunity, take it. If you are a leader with the decision-making power to plan an in-person gathering, consider doing so. You may find that your employees leave in-person events more engaged with their company and teams.

A certain subset of people don't believe that in-person meetings are meaningful. These people reason that they already have meaningful working relationships with their colleagues via remote channels and that meeting in person adds nothing to their engagement level. This may be true for you. However, it may not be true for everyone in your company. The colleague who takes everything you say the wrong way may understand you much better after sitting next to you at dinner. The manager who is about to create a new role on her team may suggest you apply after chatting with you in the breakfast line. That isn't to suggest that you need to have something brilliant and innovative to say to everyone you meet, but to make the most out of this opportunity, you will want to do some advance preparation.

In a perfect world, your employer will arrange for you to meet with your colleagues virtually before an in-person meeting. How this occurs will depend on the size of the meeting and the relationship of the individuals getting together. A team of 10 people who spend every week working closely with each other will likely not need any prearranged conversation time. Bringing together a couple hundred employees, however, will. If your company doesn't arrange for you to meet colleagues in advance of an in-person meeting, you should consider doing so yourself. This may seem awkward at first, but it will be hugely valuable. Choose a few individuals and arrange a video call. Set the expectation that you can discuss anything you want: hobbies, current events, upcoming plans, or even work. The point of the call is to make it easier for you to walk up to your colleague and strike up a conversation at the in-person meeting. That's a little hard to do if, for example, you aren't sure what he looks like.

If you consider yourself an introvert, you might worry that you will struggle to be social and communicative in person, but there's no reason why you have to have a challenging experience. A little preparation can help you be successful at mixing and mingling in between formal meetings. Plan out your small talk. In some cases, you'll be able to discuss work, but you should also have some non-work topics ready: Did your colleague have to travel far to get to the meeting? How is he enjoying it thus far? Has he had a chance to explore the area? In large meetings, social mixing can almost feel like speed dating, bouncing from person to person; if you don't have a default list of topics to raise, it can be easy for two people who only have a few virtual tasks in common to suddenly go from greetings to silence. Look up relevant topics of interest and be prepared to discuss them to keep the conversation moving. This can be as simple as looking up touristy facts about the area you're staying in or as time intensive as reading articles related to your business or meeting theme and crafting bite-sized ideas to talk about.

Being prepared with a few go-to conversation topics is important. Equally important is to identify the specific people you want to interact with and what you want to accomplish in those interactions. Again, in a smaller meeting of a dozen employees, such planning might not be as crucial, as it is likely you will be able to get face time with each individual. With larger meetings, however, you will need to seek out those you wish to connect with to further your career or to strengthen a relationship. Make a list of whom you want to meet and why; then plan out how you will introduce yourself to them and what you will talk about if they don't take the lead in the conversation. In many instances, the opportunity to talk to someone important to you can come with little notice. You might see the person walking out of the elevator or standing in line for the buffet. If you don't grab them right then, you might not have the opportunity for the rest of the event. In that kind of situation, having prepared what you want to say in advance means you will create a strong in-person impression.

These opportunities can be random and infrequent, so it's also important to be prepared to create your chances. Again, you may need to work harder to create these opportunities in larger meetings. The worst thing you can do is put off chatting with a person on your list until later, as that time may never come. Take advantage of opportunities as they come up and seek them out as well. At a convention, it is perfectly fine to walk up to people as they are talking to see if you can join the conversation, which may easily enlarge to include another person. Pay attention to body language for cues as to whether you can jump in. Often you will be able to chime in on the subject at hand. In other cases, you may wish to use one of the conversation pieces you prepared ahead of time.

Remote workforce employees can be somewhat starved for these social opportunities (You can shake someone's hand! You can see how tall the other person is!), so casual interactions are very important for deepening colleague relationships. The remote worker has to be careful, though. In the world of video calls and home offices, it is entirely possible to know someone very well before ever meeting in person. This can lead to awkward situations. The colleague you banter with all day long may not be a hugger, for example. If you are, it's best to play it safe and settle for an enthusiastic handshake. You don't have enough information on which to base the decision to hug or not. If you are on the receiving end of an unwanted hug, you can sometimes forestall it by leaning back a little and quickly putting your hand up for a handshake. You can take the sting out of your refusal by making the handshake extra warm, smiling, and saying, "It's so great to finally meet you in person!"

Equally important, of course, is the way you interact in structured activities. Presentations, meetings, and discussion groups will likely occur, and success at an in-person meeting in this context relies on one thing: participation. Your colleagues, direct reports, and supervisors will have a certain way of looking at you based on the type of virtual worker you are; this impression may change when they see what kind of worker you are in person. This is your chance to make a lasting, positive impression on those around you. During presentations, take notes. In meetings, ask questions. In small discussions, take the lead where appropriate. You should plan to be visible in your participation at least once during each event of the overall meeting.

Many of my old teammates and I have moved into different roles within the company, and I know that we may end up working together again in new formations. Just as with my in-person friendships, I make it a point to keep in touch with my former peers. Scheduling occasional check-in conversations with past colleagues can not only make for nice breaks in the day, but also keep our connections strong for any future collaboration or new managerial relationships.

—Elle Mastenbrook

Ultimately, these in-person meetings are a chance for you to recharge your batteries. Working remotely is still a new thing for some people, and as more of our experiences are moved to the online world, maximizing the in-person interactions that remain becomes even more important. Where possible, companies with virtual workers should actively create opportunities for their people to meet in person. Employees need to do their part as well, taking active steps to make sure that these opportunities are as useful as possible. The work you do to prepare for in-person meetings will not only help you enjoy them more but also help you enjoy your virtual workplace more when the time comes to go back home.

Managing Past Peers

In today's ever-changing world of advanced technology, the pace of work is always increasing. Not only are jobs and responsibilities often shifting rapidly, but entire organizational charts and reporting structures reshuffle frequently. This is even more true in the remote workforce, where change doesn't mean physically moving someone's office from one place to another or creating new nameplates with new titles. In the virtual world, a big shift can often be accomplished with far less effort. This means that your colleague one day could become your supervisor the next, and vice versa.

Therefore, build relationships with your colleagues now as if a shift will happen in the future. This isn't to say that you should act like someone's supervisor or their direct report when you're not; rather it's advice to maintain your professionalism and be aware of your image throughout your interactions. It is also helpful to be aware of the strengths and weaknesses of those around you.

When you make the shift to supervising people who used to be your colleagues, you can use the good relationships you have already formed with them as a foundation for a good working relationship as their supervisor. The types of conversations you have will likely change as you move from colleague to manager, but the knowledge you gained as a colleague can help you build a better team. By knowing the strengths and weaknesses of your team ahead of time, you can work to distribute tasks to the correct people, based on what they do well or what they want to learn, ensuring the success of your team and helping your people succeed and grow. However, be careful not to pigeonhole someone. Just because you know a person very well as a colleague doesn't mean you know how he performs specific tasks. The colleague who told you an amusing story six months ago about a spectacular failure with spreadsheets may have spent the last four months increasing this skill.

When new roles open up, many of your colleagues may apply, and you may wind up being managed by a colleague who received the role you wanted. Your prior knowledge of your colleague can give you insight into how your strengths and experiences can help the new team get a strong start and define your role within it. Be prepared to give your new manager a break—she likely feels as awkward as you do in the new relationship.

In the continuous change that is sometimes present in the remote workforce, you may even experience a shift back and forth. Someone who managed a project you worked on could become someone you manage on the next project. Or it may be the case that these two projects are going on at the same time. In the span of a single workday, you may find that you have to address the same person as your colleague, as her indirect project manager, and as an indirect report for a project she manages. In these cases, building in cues can help you shift roles. Some have found that simply saying, "I'm putting on my project manager hat for a moment," can help everyone effectively switch gears.

From the very beginning of your time in the remote workforce, maintain your professionalism and treat everyone you work with with respect. Build good relationships with your colleagues and learn their strengths and weaknesses. All of this information will help you in the future, whether you remain colleagues, begin to report to them, or become their manager.

Dealing with People Who Take Credit for Your Work

My team shares email templates, tools, and ideas on a weekly basis, and we take care to model proper attribution when talking amongst ourselves or with a wider audience. We make sharing credit a regular practice to help avoid misattribution or confusion in the first place.

In management, and even in the remote workforce more broadly, attributing ideas and work to others where appropriate demonstrates that we collaborate with our direct reports and colleagues, and that we recognize and act on constructive feedback. When I bring an idea to my director from someone who reports to me, it reinforces my credibility as a manager, someone who builds up my employees and recognizes strengths.

—Caitlin Duke

Popular culture often presents working in an office as a cutthroat affair, where it's everybody for themselves as they attempt to climb the corporate ladder. While reality is typically more mundane, sometimes people will take credit for other people's work. Office politics and misinformation have always existed, but in the virtual work environment, things become even murkier. You need greater vigilance to make sure others don't take credit for your contributions. You also need to be aware of how much easier it is to accidentally attribute credit to the wrong person and to be wary about unintentionally receiving credit for the work of others.

The main challenge in properly crediting work is the high volume of information that remote employees have to process every day. In a more traditional office, the pace tends to be slower, and there are more opportunities for face-to-face communication; therefore, when information is written, people can more easily pay attention and keep track of it. But in the remote workforce, the high volume of written information can make it challenging to find the original source of an idea. If someone steals your work, will you even be able to remember whether you first brought up the idea in a conversation over video, typed it in an instant message, or sent it through an email? The amount of information you need to process is the first major stumbling block when it comes to protecting your ideas from theft and protecting yourself from inadvertently stealing someone else's idea.

The other major obstacle is multitasking. While traditionally the ability to multitask has been something to praise, in the remote workforce attempting to multitask can be a weakness. Checking email during a meeting, bouncing from one instant messenger conversation to another, and having several open tabs in your browser is incredibly commonplace in the virtual world. Unfortunately, we know that in many cases when you multitask this way, you are more likely to produce lower-quality work. It's easy to see how this can lead to incorrectly giving credit for ideas and work: An idea gets brought up in a fast-paced email chain. A few messages down, someone accidentally attributes that idea to someone else. The person who came up with the idea might not notice, because he is also multitasking. With no objection and clarification, the ownership of that idea becomes widely attributed to the wrong person. It's possible that this wrong person takes advantage of the situation in an unethical way and doesn't point out the error. However, it's equally possible that this person has forgotten what happened earlier in the email chain, and because everyone assumes he came up with the idea, accepts it as his own.

Technology blurs the lines of ownership further. While this is something that all modern-day workers must contend with, it has a much greater impact on remote workers. When asking for help from a boss or colleague, you often end up with a written response that you can cut and paste to pass on, perhaps to answer the question that prompted you to reach out to your coworker to begin with. While many employees will not blatantly lift ideas from someone else for a high-visibility project, casual plagiarism is more likely. How are you to know whether an email you receive is one that was crafted especially for you? Perhaps your colleague simply copied the majority of it from another person in order to save time or appear more authoritative or knowledgeable. Maybe she didn't want to make a mistake interpreting a policy, so she used language from another source that she knows is accurate. In many cases this is not an issue, but it does muddy the waters of what information is original and what has been borrowed from another source. When it comes time to collaborate on projects with others, this habit can result in pinching ideas, whether intentionally or not. Be aware of this trap to avoid falling into it.

What do you do if you realize that your idea has been taken by someone else? First, look for proof. After all, you could be mistaken. Do the due diligence to find the source of the idea. You can then choose whether or not to raise the issue. Although you don't need proof to do so, addressing the issue without hard evidence to back it up increases the potential of an awkward conversation. In many cases, you won't want to confront the person who took your idea. It might not be worth it, depending on the value of the idea. Simply telling your boss may be enough. In other cases, you will need to be vocal to a wider audience to get credit for your contributions.

Escalate your concerns as appropriate. Before you do so, be clear on how the theft occurred and what you hope to accomplish by pointing it out. Take into account the fact that you may be dealing with someone of a higher rank, that raising this concern might not result in any changes, and that if you wait too long to raise your concern, there may be little anyone can do to rectify it.

The situation is slightly less murky if you are dealing with an incident in which the wrong person has been given credit for actual work done instead of just an idea. In those cases, it is often, but not always, easy to establish who did what. If you weren't given credit for the work that you did, it is often best to assume that this was a simple mistake. What you do about it depends on the situation and the people involved. In some cases you can quickly correct the statement. In others, you may need the help of your boss or another, higher-ranking person. Furthermore, if someone wrongly gives you credit for work you did not do, be quick to call out the right person. It is often easier for the person who has wrongly been given credit to rectify the situation than for the wronged party to call it out.

The virtual work environment dramatically affects how we receive and process information. It brings to mind the stories of how multiple eyewitnesses will see the same event in dramatically different, even conflicting ways. Slowing down will help you avoid missing information. Taking the time to record and organize your ideas and projects in a coherent way will allow you to give credit where it is due and determine whether someone has taken credit for something you created. With vigilance and persistence, you can keep better control of your work and what happens to it.

Parenting in the Remote Workforce

Working remotely has allowed me to be very present in my daughter's formative years while still maintaining a meaningful and successful career. I shop for groceries on weekday mornings between school drop-off and the start of my workday and volunteer for lunch duty in the school cafeteria once a month. I take my daughter to school every morning and pick her up every afternoon, and I am here to help her with homework questions in between my afternoon meetings.

I also keep solid boundaries between my work and home lives by planning in advance when my workday will end and sticking to it. This means I not only get to structure my day to be available to my daughter while also being productive, but I also enjoy uninterrupted time with my family every evening.

—Dru Ciotti

Although there are remote workforce positions that allow you to complete your work while parenting your children all day, there is a very good chance that you do not have one of these jobs. If a company's workforce is primarily remote, then it may even have guidelines that explicitly state that parents must arrange child care during work hours. This chapter assumes that your company has such a policy and that you have taken steps to arrange appropriate child care.

Having children adds an additional layer to all aspects of life, including the remote work experience. You work from home. You live at home. Your children also live in your home. As a worker and a parent, you have to deal with not only the logistics that come with this reality but also the assumptions that others in your company may make about you and your work ethic.

No matter how well you have arranged your child care and workspace, at some point your child is going to intrude into your work life. If you have a small apartment and child care in the home, kid noises in other rooms may be loud enough to be heard on a call. Some remote workers have had children knock on locked office doors, loudly demanding justice or juice. It does not matter that their caregiver was closer and available to deal with the situation. It does not matter that you told little Sophie that when the work door is closed, Daddy can't talk. At some point, children forget that work hours are for working. You will always be their parent first.

You are not immune to this issue if your child care is outside of your home. Employees work across multiple time zones in the remote workforce. Inevitably someone you can't refuse is going to ask for a meeting outside of your work hours. Since the call is outside your normal workday, you may not be required to have child care, but you likely still want to maintain a professional space for your professional interaction.

While you can't eliminate all child intrusions, you can take steps to minimize them. Many parents have found that sound-canceling headphones help with noise. If your child is preschool aged or older, strong visual cues can help. Some parents have put a line of tape on the floor to denote where children have to stop in Mommy's office in order to not be on camera. Other parents have installed locks or stop signs on an office door. If the problem is noise in an echoing hallway, consider ways to muffle the echo. Perhaps a few small rugs can help. Consistent reminders and role-playing can also help children develop the habit of leaving you to your work during work hours.

Dealing with children's intrusions is straightforward, and although you may have to spend some time thinking through a workable solution, you can tell when you arrive at one. The same can't be said about other people's assumptions. A small percentage of people will assume that you are watching your children instead of doing your job. It isn't always clear who may think this, but the assumptions largely come from people who have not dealt with similar intrusions themselves. This could be people new to the remote environment, traditional office workers, or those who are childless.

It can be disheartening to have your professionalism called into question, but fight the impulse to say something intemperate. Often these accusations come as a surprise, since you know you followed the rules. It's important to realize that accusations often come from a place of ignorance. A director in an office in a different time zone may not have thought through the logistical consequences of calling a last-minute meeting at 7:00 a.m. your time, if it is 10:00 a.m. for everyone else. You may have told your boss that your children will be home during the meeting, but the director heading the call may not have received that message.

Where appropriate, you may wish to reach out directly to explain that you can attend said meeting at the designated time, but that the meeting is outside of your normal work hours so your children will be at home. While you have plans in place for your children during your regular work hours, those plans do not extend to your personal time. Your home office is your only office, and the children live in the home. If it is not appropriate for you to reach out, then make sure your boss or another appropriate person does so in your stead. Seasoned remote workers will understand that the personal side of an employee's life sometimes blends with the professional. Traditional office workers will not automatically understand the consequences of meetings held outside of work hours. If you assume that you need to make this clear, then you can minimize the number of misunderstandings and rude surprises.

If the person making assumptions about your work ethic holds a higher position in the company than you do, it is often most effective for your manager or someone of a higher position to act as your advocate. This is especially true if your advocate has a positive relationship with the person making assumptions.

Your strategy needs to be more nuanced if your boss is the one who thinks you are watching your children all day instead of working. Take some time to stop and think about why your boss may believe this. Perhaps you recently became a parent. Perhaps a child intruded on an important meeting. If this is the case, did your boss know you had a child before the child intruded? This may seem like an absurd question, but if you're very good at keeping your children separate from your workspace and you don't speak about your children at work, then that intrusion may have been the first indication your boss had that there are children in your home.

No matter the reason, data can be your advocate. Does your boss agree that your role requires an employee who is focused on the work, rather than watching children? Does she agree that you get your work done on time? Are you finishing things slower than your colleagues or generally at the same rate? Do you turn in quality deliverables? If you were secretly watching your children instead of working, wouldn't that become obvious in your performance? You may also wish to explain your child care arrangements. It's worth reiterating that your child care plans cover your normal working hours, and while you may be willing and able to take calls outside of those hours, your current lifestyle does not support live-in, continuous child care. Above all else, keep your temper and lead with patience.

The remote workforce can present challenges for the working parent. Fortunately, the benefits far outweigh the occasional misunderstanding. The majority of remote employees understand and celebrate the flexibility that comes with the remote lifestyle. Many parents have found that they can more easily attend a school play or field trip because they have the power to make up those hours in the evening after the children go to bed. Eliminating the long commute to and from the office may mean that your family can eat dinner together during the week. You may see your children more often. Enjoy your flexibility, and remember to be transparent with those who may see or hear your children. With some forethought and communication, you can enjoy the benefits that the remote setting has to offer parents and minimize any difficulties.

Staying in the Loop

In any workplace, it's important to keep up with the latest news. This isn't about gossip but rather the important updates and announcements that come with working at any organization. People change roles or leave the organization all the time. Policies, rules, and standard operating procedures can change just as often. In a traditional working environment, you can often absorb this kind of information just by being in the same room as others: It's easy to make announcements to large groups of people at once, and open floor plans allow for quick and easy movement of information.

In the remote workforce, however, it's not as easy. Information comes in many forms, and it usually has to be formally shared to ensure that everyone is updated. The volume of communication in the virtual work environment is such that it is relatively easy for employees not to process new information in a timely manner. While this can be limited to employees feeling surprised and perhaps a bit left out, it can also lead to significant mistakes, miscommunication, or even accidental security breaches.

To avoid being the last person to find out important company news, you need to be proactive. Build into your schedule a daily or weekly review of your inbox, group communications, and any other location where updates are shared. Set aside 30 minutes at the end of your week to sift through announcements to make sure that you have not missed anything important. Prioritize emails that come from individuals who often make important announcements so you read those messages before they get buried in your inbox. Your inclination may be to first take care of tasks that have more action associated with them, but reviewing these info-laden emails in a timely manner can greatly help you in the long term.

It's also important to start wide. Make sure that, where possible and appropriate, you are part of many mailing lists and online work communities related to your position to get a sense of what value each provides. Then trim the fat, removing yourself from those that are not as valuable or that provide duplicate information. It can be tempting to avoid signing up for another group to keep your email volume down, but that new group might actually do the job of two other groups you are already a part of. Test out new information channels as they come along and then pragmatically cut loose the ones that don't provide timely information.

One of the best ways I've found for keeping myself in the loop is to stay curious about other departments, and news that affects them. I try to take a regular look at the current openings posted on the company's internal jobs website. I also make it a point to read the articles people post in the different distribution channels at work, and sometimes post comments and follow-up questions in the thread. I try to act as if I might have to work in that department some day. Doing so has led to a couple of positive outcomes. First, it helps me to remain nimble—when territories and duties change at work, I've already taken that first step toward familiarizing myself with the my new tasks. I also have a high-level handle on some of the issues I may have to deal with. Secondly, people are more likely to talk to you if you've been an active participant in a shared chat. This helps me to have a sense of who to reach out to for different things, and because my name is familiar, they are more apt to open my email!

—*Teresa Douglas*

Information also comes more quickly to those who have opportunities to communicate with others. If you are always on the passive end of a relationship, there's no reason for you to get news outside of highly formal channels, which can often be the last ones to share changes and updates. Being an active communicator is important in general in the remote workforce, but it's especially important if you want to find out information first. Talking to different individuals on a regular basis will allow you to find out what is happening on their end, and news will travel to you more quickly. Regular communication will also help you home in on those select individuals who are privy to the most up-to-date info.

Information is a valuable commodity in any workplace. If you stay apprised of what's going on, then you are more likely to be approached with requests for help, viewed as an important member of the team, and considered for promotions and other opportunities. You are also more likely to feel equipped to handle times of change and transition. Be proactive and engaged, and you will not only know more before others but also become someone whom others go to for updates and clarification.

Working with On-Site Team Members or On a Partially On-Site Team

The more a business grows, the more potential there is for conflict. Even the best-run operation will see some level of conflict, because human beings are very good at drawing lines between themselves and others, and this tendency exists in the remote workforce as well. Perhaps the most interesting dynamic in the remote workforce occurs when an organization has a set of employees who only work from home and a set who always, or nearly always, work in a more traditional office environment.

People who work from home need to be sensitive to the fact that their on-site colleagues will likely assume that the grass is greener on the other side. They may picture their remote colleagues as living the good life: working in pajamas, sleeping in, and taking as many breaks as they want because there is no boss watching from across the room. Although some remote employees take advantage of one, some, or all of these perceived perks, making the assumption that those who work from home are lazy is incorrect and unfair. That said, it's important to recognize that many on-site colleagues will assume the worst, so try not to take offense when they do. Conflict arises when both sides start accusing each other of having it easier.

Along the same lines, remote workers should resist the urge to talk about the advantages that working from home brings. Seemingly innocuous comments, such as "I did the laundry on my lunch break," can come across as bragging. While in a perfect world, people wouldn't have to be this concerned about what they say to colleagues, savvy virtual employees will choose their words carefully and be aware that any resentment that on-site coworkers display is likely not personal.

This kind of problem can also occur when individuals vent about the frustrating elements of their day. While venting is an essential part of managing one's work life, you have to choose the proper time and place and be aware of the people you're with when sharing your frustrations. Even when those frustrations may sound to your ears like reasons why working from home is not always desirable, they can be interpreted in the wrong way. A complaint about the noise your family has been making all day while you're trying to work is a valid concern, but to an on-site coworker's ears, it may simply serve as a reminder of how little time he gets to spend with his family. Instead, focus on the work itself and the projects at hand to avoid misinterpretations. When it comes to casual conversation (the kind that usually occurs at the start of calls), keep it more neutral and avoid using your place of work as a talking point.

In meetings where there is a mix of virtual and on-site employees and the responsibilities of the two groups differ, it's important to be mindful of meeting topics. If a discussion is only relevant for one subset of the group, it can serve to deepen the divide between on-site and off-site workers. In general, people shouldn't be forced to sit through large portions of meetings that don't apply to them.

There are other steps to take during meetings to ensure everyone's participation is balanced. Something as simple as how the meeting is set up can greatly affect how the different teams see each other—literally. Set up ground rules in advance to avoid dividing the teams in obvious ways. All team members should be on camera if possible, regardless of whether they are on the call from the office or not. If all the remote workers are on camera, while on-site colleagues are together in a conference room and only on audio, it creates two distinct groups. Similarly, it's just as problematic if all on-site workers are together and on a single camera. Aside from the volume and visibility issues this setup can create, it again highlights the difference between the two groups; it sends a visual message that the on-site team is a separate group, rather than several individuals who are part of the larger team. The point is to avoid distinguishing different types of people on the call and to ensure that everyone can hear and participate so that the meeting is as efficient as possible.

There is an art to contributing in meetings where some people are remote and others are on-site. No matter how deeply committed your colleagues are to including you in the discussion, the on-site group will unconsciously bias toward listening to the people who are on-site. You have to be quick with your unmute button and take advantage of any micro pause in the conversation to add your contribution. There seems to be a larger cognitive load attached to listening to the person who is on-screen. The clearer and more targeted you can make your words, the more chance you have of being understood and integrated into the conversation.

—Sascha Strelka

As a remote worker, it is wise to be prepared for situations that exclude you. For example, there may be a party upon the completion of a project that includes food or drink, which you cannot participate in because you are a virtual employee. Someone may have a baby shower and forget to invite the virtual employees. Do your best to not be offended and instead focus on solutions. If you know there will be a celebration that virtual employees are not invited to, reach out to the meeting organizer to discuss ways virtual employees can attend: Maybe the party can be held in a conference room with video calling set up. Maybe food or drinks can be sent to the virtual employees who participated in the project, or they can buy their own and then expense them. Don't be afraid to reach out after the fact as well, to discuss ways virtual employees could be included in the future.

It's equally important to establish with your on-site colleagues that you, as a remote worker, are still very much part of the team and whatever projects are underway. To this end, make sure you are a part of all meetings that are relevant to you and your role. It's easy for on-site project leaders or supervisors to grab employees who are physically in front of them for an impromptu meeting on something that a remote teammate would also find useful. Be proactive: Talk to these leaders so this doesn't become the norm and so you are looped in as a full participant, in whatever way makes the most sense. Ensure that assignments are set with clear deadlines, or at the very least, tell your on-site counterparts what you'll be doing and when you'll have your work completed. Even though they can't see you working, they'll know you're getting your share done and hitting your deadlines. You may also need to compromise when it comes to your schedule, making sure you're available and online when your colleagues in the office are working on your shared projects or tasks. That way, they can easily reach out to you with questions and requests and get a response right away, just as though you were down the hall. The goal is to reduce the impression that you, as a remote worker, are somehow different from everyone else in ways that matter to the team.

When an organization goes fully remote with its workforce, employees face many challenges. But when a company has a workforce split between off- and on-site, there are additional and slightly different considerations. Fair or not, those who work virtually will often have to make the majority of accommodations. Most remote employees have worked in an office, whereas most on-site folks have not worked remotely. That means the onus is on those who work virtually to be sensitive to their colleagues' potential lack of awareness of what it means to work from home. The result will be a more harmonious workforce, which can only be a positive for everyone involved, regardless of the physical location where they work.

The Person Who Has the Option of Working from Home

Some employees work at a physical location that they need to commute to every day. Others work from home and never need to go anywhere as part of their work. Yet other employees work from home some of the time and spend the rest of the time out in the field, visiting clients, performing inspections, and doing other tasks that can only be done in person. There is still another group of workers: those who have the option to work either at home or in an office. This group can potentially be seen as having the best of both worlds. They can take advantage of the benefits of both types of work life while avoiding some of the negatives that each side can bring. Naturally it's not as cut-and-dried as that, and there are many factors these workers need to take into account to do what is best for them and the company they work for.

When deciding whether or not to work from home on any particular day, it's important to understand your supervisor's (and company's) expectations. There may be official rules, which of course make the decision much easier. However, in most cases expectations are unwritten or very general. Learn how much time a person in your position can acceptably work from home and make sure you understand how to notify your supervisor about where you'll be. The last thing you want is for your boss to feel that you're not in the office enough, which can result in distrust. The same goes for coworkers' expectations. If you're working remotely four days a week, while all your colleagues are working from home just one day a week, you may be sending the wrong message. "He's just never here!" is not something you want your supervisor or your coworkers to think. Following both official and unofficial policies helps avoid this issue.

Some of the reasons why you may want to work from home are better than others. Maybe there are personal reasons that keep you from the office but don't require you to take a personal day or time off. Perhaps there's a delivery that you need to be at home to receive. Or maybe your teenager is sick and needs someone to remind her to take her medicine every four hours. These reasons are generally accepted by colleagues and supervisors back at the office but can cause problems if they occur on a regular basis. Making sure that colleagues and supervisors know not just where you are but *why* you are out of the office is important to keep your working relationships harmonious.

One important reason to work from home is to increase productivity. While many people might assume that when you're at work in the office, you're getting more done, working from home usually provides an environment free from interruptions. Think about all the times when someone stops by your office or cubicle to chat and how that can interrupt your flow. You may get called into meetings you feel obligated to attend, even though they are not as pressing as the deadlines you have to meet. Many employees who have a balance of on-site and off-site work locations comment on how much more productive they are when working from home. They can clear their inboxes and work on projects for long stretches at a time, rarely putting tasks on pause.

Timing is also key when deciding which days to remain in the office. While there may be pressing reasons to work from home at certain times, there are also strong reasons to be in the office at other times. There could be important visitors coming to your floor or building, making your physical presence advantageous. Maybe these visitors are a big part of your work duties—collaborators on a project, for example—or maybe they are senior management and you want them to see you working hard. If you're at home, they won't be able to see you in action, and your absence could even be viewed in a negative light. This is especially true if the visit was planned in advance, as most such visits are. Your absence easily raises the question "Why isn't she here on this particular day? Didn't she know we were coming?" It's also important to be present for meetings about big projects you are directly involved with or that you will indirectly be affected by. For situations in which several colleagues or teams often work remotely, there is real value in making sure you are in the office when they are on-site as well so you have the opportunity to interact in person. On the other hand, it may make more sense for you to be in the office when they are gone to provide any needed support in their absence. Make sure you not only have good reasons for working from home but also understand the appropriate times to work from the office.

I used to make it a point to attend all big meetings in person, even though I worked from home.

Home was under two hours away from the office, and it was easier for me to feel socially comfortable actually meeting people in person instead of over a video call. Once I knew a number of people in the office, I didn't feel the need to be physically present at all of the meetings anymore.

—Sascha Strelka

Another important reason to show up at the office on a regular basis is to take full advantage of the "water cooler" moments you can miss out on when working from home. In an organization that is completely remote, your colleagues will probably work together to intentionally re-create such moments, but in an environment where people can choose to work virtually from time to time, you are unlikely to have any sense of the atmosphere of the office while at home. Therefore, it's imperative that you take opportunities to go into the office to get a sense of the organizational culture and strengthen your connections with colleagues through informal interactions. Eat your lunch with others. Visit your colleagues in person and discuss current projects. Have an actual "water cooler" moment at the office's water cooler. Really consider what you want to accomplish by coming into the office. Perhaps a coworker is giving a presentation and your presence, though perhaps not business-critical, would show moral support. Make sure you have a list of important dates for the people you work with. Recognizing birthdays or a colleague's return from an extended leave can strengthen the bonds among you. For someone who more often works from home, being strategic about on-site visits is an important part of being a successful employee.

With the right mindset, employees who have the option to work both in the office and from home can make their jobs extremely rewarding. They can more easily manage the work-life balance that many remote workforce employees sometimes struggle with. They can increase job satisfaction and productivity. They can truly achieve the best of both worlds. That said, there is no default setting. These types of employees need to make careful decisions about when and where they work and how to present the right image to their colleagues and supervisors. If they accomplish this, their careers will greatly benefit.

Chapter 7

Secrets for Managers

The chapters in this section are written for managers with remote direct reports. They contain the hard-won knowledge of those who came before you. These are the things your employees wish you knew.

Is It Really So Different?

> I quickly learned that relationship building is of primary importance in remote management. When I first started in this role, I focused on clarifying key responsibilities and setting goals, which in my previous experience had been the definition of successful management.
>
> While those steps are still extremely important, I found that as the manager of remote employees, I did not naturally have the relationship with my team to bring out the best in them. I didn't learn about their lives outside of work the way I might have just by being in physical proximity. In a shared office, you see photos of families on desks, have small talk around the water cooler or vending machines, and exchange stories while grabbing coffee or lunch. In a remote environment, I was missing the personal context to help me understand my employees' challenges and priorities.
>
> That's why I now start every new managerial relationship by asking about my new employee's life, family, and interests, and take the time to share about myself, too. This relationship building gives me a firmer basis for challenging my employees—they know I care about who they are as people, and not just how their output benefits me and our organization.
>
> —Dustin Semo

One of the trickiest parts of managing in the remote environment is that it can seem so similar to a traditional office. There are still meetings to run, deadlines to meet, and company initiatives to implement. The sales team still needs to meet its targets, operations employees need to make sure everything runs on time, and someone in finance needs to pay the bills. All of these similarities can lull a manager into thinking that a managerial style that works in a traditional office will translate well into the remote world. However, the savvy manager will realize that the two environments are not the same and take steps to manage effectively in this setting.

To even begin to understand the enormity of the differences, consider this: In an on-site office, managers constantly receive feedback (both overt and subliminal) without even realizing it. Let's say Joe is managing a team and makes a bad decision about something (or maybe the decision is right, but the delivery is poor). The office goes quiet. People look down or start to fidget. Joe's discussions with team members are met with shorter, clipped responses. Employee Sally, who never goes to lunch and is always the last to leave the office, not only goes to lunch with five others but also leaves work an hour early claiming to have a headache. In short, Joe is handed a mass of tacit feedback from his employees that the decision is not being accepted well.

Now let's look at the same situation in the remote world, where management is still operating in an office-traditional way. Joe in Hartford calls Sally in Chicago and makes the same announcement as in the above example. In a remote office, what will Sally do? She'll likely feel isolated, without any colleagues with whom she can blow off steam. She might tell her significant other or a family member about the frustration she feels, or perhaps she'll take a quick walk around her neighborhood to cool off. At some point, though, she'll likely call her friend and coworker Larry in Seattle to consult or vent a little. More than likely, Larry then calls Lynn in Denver, who calls Jane in Memphis, who . . . You get the idea. Potentially in just a few hours, 20 people in the organization know that Joe has a problem. But who is the one person in the country who doesn't know? That's right: Joe.

This is just one example of the new order and new understanding that are necessary to ensure a happy, engaged remote workforce—not in terms of the need for a different hierarchy or reporting matrix (which we take as a given), but in how that hierarchy or matrix needs to function. Information flows in new and sometimes unpredictable ways in the remote world. Conversations in this environment are fundamentally different from those that occur in an actual office, where follow-up and context can be provided as necessary. Interpersonal relationships are crafted and developed in unique ways remotely. Career pathing for individuals has to be inspired and discussed differently. Company culture is not absorbed as it is in the office environment, so hiring and training must incorporate and reinforce this explicitly.

The old management guidebook might have been great in a Madison Avenue office, but in the remote workforce, we need a different map.

To Be Heard

When I first started as a manager, one of my colleagues told me how important it was to check in with each of my direct reports every day. I looked at my packed calendar, which had maybe 10 minutes of free time on it almost every day of the week and asked, "How?"

She said, "It's easy. Just send a chat. 'Hi, how are you? How's your day?'"

It was such a simple piece of advice, but so important. I get incredible energy from time with my own manager. I love the opportunity to talk about what I'm working on, get their perspective, and gain more confidence. The result is that I do my best, and I feel great about it.

So, I made it my mission to check in with everyone in some way every single day. Sometimes it's because we have our regular one-on-one meeting scheduled. Sometimes, it's just a quick chat to say "Hey, how are things?" Sometimes it's meeting with two or three of my reports as we work through a problem together.

One day, I started what I thought would be a quick check-in chat and quickly got 15 messages in response. I immediately told my next meeting that I needed some time to talk to my team member. Once we hopped into a video chat, we solved our problem in the first five minutes, and spent the rest of our time catching up about her life outside of work.

By making myself fully available to my team, I frequently catch needs like these before they balloon, and also get to know my direct reports better.

—Kate Mitsakis

For many people, the idea of an absent or mostly silent boss sounds like an ideal situation. For the remote worker, however, a silent boss isn't a positive thing. When you don't have the opportunity to see your boss roaming the halls, to notice her talking to another employee who works in a nearby office, or even to run into her while grabbing a coffee, communication becomes much more important. Your employees don't want you as someone who only exists to rubber-stamp payroll; they want to have a relationship in which their thoughts and opinions are heard and acknowledged.

The virtual workspace doesn't lend itself to silent forms of approval or recognition. Your direct report can't see you smile and nod as you read the email he sent. Without some kind of reply, he won't know whether his contribution is a good one, has some flaws, or was even seen at all. It can be disheartening for an employee to share his thoughts and never receive any acknowledgment from his boss. While providing a quick response to messages you receive from your employees is a great place to start, it's also important to really listen to what your people are asking of you. To truly be heard means more than just getting a "Thanks!" in reply. While such replies are appreciated, it's also important to sometimes send longer, more articulate responses so your people know that you are listening to what they are telling you.

Every manager knows that her employees will sometimes find themselves together and use that opportunity to talk to each other about work. They'll discuss the good parts of their jobs and the bad parts; this will be an opportunity for them to raise their thoughts and opinions of their work life and receive validation from their colleagues. This scenario is harder to come by in the remote workforce, so as the boss, you will need to take proactive steps to ensure that it occurs. A boss in an on-site office can lock herself away behind a closed door and at least know that her employees will be able to talk to each other without too much effort. A remote boss who does the same thing risks isolating her employees. Fortunately, there are many things you can do to help your employees feel heard while getting your own work done. You can provide discussion-based opportunities for team members to raise ideas. For example, you could set up a system or program for your team to share ideas and brainstorm through an instant-messaging platform, or you could hold "coffee breaks" online, where you meet an employee or a group of employees for a short period to chat about any topics (work related or not).

It's also important to make sure your direct reports have the tools to communicate with you in more formal ways, if appropriate. A program that allows the sharing of documents can be useful for some remote workers. It makes your communication with your employees a more collaborative one, so they can see how their contributions are being recognized and used in the context of bigger discussions and projects. Many programs that allow you to share documents will also provide you with tools to make comments on contributions, further strengthening the dialogue you're building with your team.

You are your remote employees' most important link to the company. Feeling that you hear them will be a driving force for high engagement and job satisfaction. Use online tools to foster a collaborative and communicative environment where all contributions are recognized in one form or another. By doing this, you will ensure that your employees show up ready to do their best work, confident you are there to guide them along the way.

To Be Recognized

One of the most important things to know about managing employees in the remote workforce is that you need to actively show that you hear them and recognize their contributions. But to be an effective manager, you have to go one step further: You need to sing their praises. Like most people, employees want to have that pat on the back, and often they want that recognition to be public to some degree. Remote workers in particular may crave this type of recognition because so often their hard work is only visible to themselves. As a manager in this environment, you need to take more overt steps to show recognition than you would in a traditional office setting.

When considering the best ways to recognize your employees, remember that large- and small-scale rituals are equally important. Examples of large-scale recognition are taking part in a formal awards process or highlighting your employees' significant accomplishments during an all-in meeting. Small-scale options include taking the time to celebrate a minor success during your one-on-one call or a smaller group meeting. If you only focus on the large-scale recognition, your opportunities will be fewer and further between. You may also find yourself lumping together several examples of success by multiple employees in order to cover everyone, which diminishes the value of the recognition. Similarly, if small-scale recognition is the sole avenue of delivery, you risk your employees feeling like their contributions are not worthy enough to be shared more widely. The solution is to provide a mix of both approaches.

At the beginning of every division-wide meeting, we take 10 minutes to learn about the "movers and shakers" in our work community. Each individual who has moved to a new area of the company is named and celebrated, and we hear testimonials about the people and teams who have made a difference in the business over the previous quarter. This practice is a fixture that allows all of us to publicly recognize one another's accomplishments, and the commitment of time demonstrates that our place of work values us and our contributions.

—Caitlin Duke

It's also important to realize that different people like to be recognized differently. You may have someone who truly feels uncomfortable in the spotlight and may not appreciate being called out in the middle of a large meeting, even though the news being shared is positive. Another employee might appreciate the value of small-scale recognition but yearn for his exploits to be more widely broadcast to his peers. Without that, he may feel like he's not getting his name out there and that he doesn't have the chance to build a network or create a viable career path with the company. Consider individual preferences and weigh the type of recognition you show toward those preferences when possible.

In the remote workforce, you have to consciously bestow praise more than you would in an in-person office environment. There are fewer casual interactions and, as a result, fewer unplanned opportunities to recognize your employee for a job well done. It's easy to think, "Didn't I just praise this person last week? Do I really need to look for something else to say about how well they're doing?" The answer is yes. While it may seem forced at first, you're helping to build a better work environment for your employee by filling in the gaps in interaction with positive recognition. It's also important to note that in the remote workforce, a lot of your communication with employees is likely to be in the form of writing, and while praise in the written word is certainly powerful and people appreciate having their successes documented, hearing the recognition directly from one's boss through a video or audio meeting can be even more powerful.

Recognition is a must for the success of any manager of remote employees. If giving regular, consistent recognition isn't second nature for you, develop a system to help you to remember to do so. The more you practice giving praise, the more naturally it will come. You will find the increase in happiness and productivity of your employees will make it well worth the effort.

To Be Given Flexibility

Nothing makes me feel like I've won the job lottery quite so much as running in the woods on a Tuesday afternoon. While other office workers have to stare out the window at the rare sunny days we get in Vancouver, I get to pound through forest trails, surrounded by old-growth Douglas fir trees.

A portion of my work can be done at any time of day or night, allowing me to create extended breaks on certain days. I know that my running break makes me a more empathetic colleague and a better problem solver. It's also a great way to ward off the afternoon slump.

Even more importantly, my director recognizes and celebrates the flexibility of the remote workforce by taking breaks himself. If he is going on a field trip with his son, he'll tell us about it in the team chat. If he has a doctor's appointment, he'll tell us when he's coming back. This kind of transparency creates an environment where the team feels safe to take breaks and talk about what we do outside of work.

—*Teresa Douglas*

One of the biggest selling points of working remotely is the flexibility that it can offer. Different teams have different needs that will determine the extent of flexibility that is realistic, but generally speaking, the remote world allows for more flexibility than does an on-site office. If that flexibility could exist but doesn't, you may end up with employees who are frustrated with their work situation. Even if you tell them (and yourself) that the rules you're laying down are no different from those that employees in a traditional office environment need to follow, your remote employees will soon realize that it's not the same at all.

The first step is to simply accept, allow, and encourage flexibility in your workforce, as appropriate. This doesn't mean that there are no rules and no accountability, though you will have to relinquish some control. To promote appropriate flexibility, you need to be transparent with your reports regarding what is allowed and how they should keep you informed about managing their own time and deliverables. If you provide clear communication and firm expectations about the flexibility your team has at its disposal, then you should not experience problems. If you are not firm about your expectations or are too firm about limiting flexibility, then you will struggle to manage your remote team.

The biggest contribution you can make to your employees' flexibility is being open to a nontraditional work structure. Expecting your reports to always sign in by a certain time and work a set number of hours per day, even if they are nonexempt employees, is going to make your remote workforce feel stifled. Working remotely comes with its own set of challenges, but it also comes with unique benefits, a big one being a flexible work schedule. Denying your employees this flexibility makes no sense and will actively lower their engagement. The focus should be on getting tasks done in a timely manner and less on precisely when those tasks are being accomplished.

Your actions should also back up your words. It's not going to work to say that your team has the flexibility to arrange their schedules in ways that make sense for them, but then set things up so they effectively lose that flexibility. Scheduling meetings is a big issue here. In a traditional office setting, the boss can walk into a shared workspace and see that all of her reports are present and not currently on calls. She can then announce a quick meeting and ask everyone to go into the boardroom for updates. While one can argue about the value of ad hoc meetings even in a traditional office environment, it's far worse for remote workers. You cannot see what all your employees are engaged in, so you should avoid last-minute meetings. If you regularly call last-minute meetings, then your team will feel obligated to make themselves available at all times, thereby reducing their flexibility. Even providing a day's notice is not ideal unless you have pressing matters that cannot be effectively conveyed in another form of communication. Your employees likely have existing meetings set up with clients or perhaps their own direct reports, so sudden requests for meetings can impact your organization in larger ways than you might expect. Plan your meetings out in advance and make good use of a system, such as a shared calendar app, whereby you can see your employees' availability. This will ensure regular meetings happen at appropriate times and the occasional emergency meeting happens with minimal inconvenience. Finally, make sure your team knows it's OK if they can't make these sudden meetings; provide them with notes or some other form of a recap so they don't feel like they're missing out.

You should also make sure that you are honoring the spirit of the flexible work schedule. It doesn't work to provide your employees the option of taking the afternoon off to pick up their kids from school if during that time you're sending messages marked "urgent" or calling them with questions that could wait until they are back in the office. Your employees should feel like they are truly able to flex their schedules without being tied to their phone or laptop to meet your needs. This may require you to adjust your own schedule to ensure you can ask any pressing questions before your employee leaves for the remainder of the afternoon. Additionally, you should demonstrate how you yourself use the flexible work schedule as a way to encourage your employees to do the same. Provide quick updates on how you're leaving "the office" to pick up your child from school and how you'll be staying later in the evening to catch up on anything that needs to be done.

Recognizing that your employees in the remote workforce need flexibility in order to get the most out of their job is crucial. It ultimately comes down to trust. You should trust that they will get their jobs done based on the expectations that were set when they were hired or when your organization went remote, as well as the expectations that you set every time you talk to them about the team's goals. Make flexibility a selling point and then commit to it. Not only accept but encourage nontraditional work schedules, and support them by making the meetings and deadlines you set for your team fit within this framework. You may initially feel like you're losing control over your employees, but you're actually gaining far more—their trust, their commitment, and their longevity.

To Be Engaged

Engagement in the workforce has steadily become a more visible and important topic for businesses. The correlation between a happy and engaged workforce and a company's bottom line is a strong one, so many businesses are putting more effort into ensuring that employees are having a good experience with their jobs. This activity requires a fair amount of energy and attention from those in management, and when it comes to the remote workforce, it requires even greater vigilance.

It's not just company profits that are at stake; the fact is that virtual employees can move to another company more easily, taking their expertise with them and forcing your company to incur the expense of replacing them. If your employees have experience working remotely, they can look for other jobs without being restricted to a particular city or even a country in some cases. While you should be invested in your people enough to want them to be engaged simply because you care about them, the fact that many of your employees are less locked into their job than those in a traditional office should weigh heavily in your consideration as well.

So how do you engage your remote workforce? Stay in contact. There's more to it than just that, of course, but if you make it your goal to be in regular contact with your people, you will be more likely to ensure they feel engaged. This contact is best achieved through consistent check-ins. You can arrange it so that you have a daily, weekly, or biweekly call with your direct reports, or you can use key events in your business to determine the appropriate timing (e.g., after certain sales cycles end). During these check-ins, you should find out what parts of their work your employees enjoy. Conversely, what type of work do they want to reduce? This information will allow you to figure out the best way to keep your team engaged, because it will allow you to modify work responsibilities where possible, based on the preferences of your employees.

The trick here is to be consistent in your connections with your employees but not to slide into the realm of micromanaging. While it's frustrating enough to have a boss who micromanages in a traditional office environment, in the remote workforce it can feel even worse, despite the lack of a physical presence. In part, this is because your remote worker expects to be trusted to do their job, so micromanaging is a violation of that trust. It's also because a ton of formal calls and emails from the boss combined with the random but always-present pings through chat and instant messages can make the employee feel like you are in their head and there's no escape.

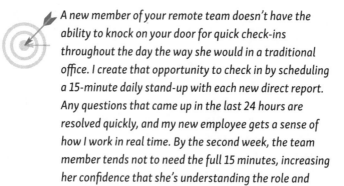

A new member of your remote team doesn't have the ability to knock on your door for quick check-ins throughout the day the way she would in a traditional office. I create that opportunity to check in by scheduling a 15-minute daily stand-up with each new direct report. Any questions that came up in the last 24 hours are resolved quickly, and my new employee gets a sense of how I work in real time. By the second week, the team member tends not to need the full 15 minutes, increasing her confidence that she's understanding the role and meeting expectations.

—*Dustin Semo*

With that in mind, a savvy manager of remote workers will assume the best of his employees. It may seem counterintuitive to keep your staff engaged by not always being there to check on what they are doing, but it will actually increase their engagement to know that their boss trusts them, especially in an environment where nobody actually sees them in action.

It's key to find a balance between consistent check-ins and micromanagement; you need to ensure that your team doesn't feel abandoned due to your efforts to show you trust them. Finding that middle path will create a greater sense of engagement for your team. Make sure your employees have ample opportunities to raise any difficulties they are facing. Remember, they won't have the convenience of running into you at the office, so you need to provide them with the opportunity instead.

It is also important to be selective about the number of initiatives you create for your employees. While part of the joy of managing people is identifying new and interesting ways to develop your team, too many initiatives can leave employees feeling pulled in too many directions, with too little time to complete their daily tasks. Especially if these initiatives regularly peter out, duplicate existing work, or fail to create change, your employees will feel the frustration of busy people who were obliged to waste their time. This can also make change management harder for you and your company. Your reports may become reluctant to fully invest in a new procedure because there is a decent chance that procedure will soon become part of the wasteland of abandoned projects and resources. In the remote workforce, evidence of those failures is more obvious and therefore easy for your direct reports to call to mind.

Employee engagement is a crucial area for any manager to master, but the manager of a remote workforce needs to find success in this area sooner than the manager of a traditional workforce. If you can find the right level of engagement, you will not only gain the financial benefits of an engaged workforce, but you'll also feel a tremendous sense of emotional satisfaction.

A Sense of Community

Within my team, we have transitioned from top-down weekly group calls into meetings led by our peers. We rotate this responsibility, which gives us a chance to focus on a wide variety of topics. And just as important as the business-related content of each call is the 10 or so minutes we spend responding to a thoughtful icebreaker that helps us continue to know one another as people. Before one team member departed for maternity leave, we threw her a virtual baby shower with a quick game, sent her an e-card we had all signed, and gave her a gift card—we had everything but the cake.

—*Caitlin Duke*

Remote workers lose so much when they leave the traditional office: long commutes, rigid work schedules, inconvenient office spaces. The list of positive losses goes on and on. As a manager, however, it's important to acknowledge the aspects of a traditional office that many workers miss. Remote employees, who for the most part have grown up associating work with leaving home and entering a ready-made world full of acquaintances, no longer have that world waiting for them when they begin their workday—unless you, as their manager, help them create it.

This sense of community is different from the relationship that your employee has with you. Your direct report needs to feel, as much as possible, that he is part of a larger team of people working for the same company and toward the same goals. In a traditional office, this occurs naturally with little effort from you: Workers are thrown together for 40 hours a week within the same physical space. In the remote world, your team may be scattered across the country—or the world—and each of them may work alone. Unless you take steps to create a community, your reports may feel as if they are freelancers working for an imaginary company.

You may already have a regular, one-on-one meeting scheduled with each of your direct reports. While that is important, it isn't sufficient for building a larger sense of community. Many managers have found that a weekly team meeting is a useful vehicle for connecting their direct reports to each other and the company at large. At the most basic level, a team meeting can help your team get to know one another so they have someone to talk to during the day. If you bring in special guests, your team can also learn more about different departments in the organization. This is helpful, as it often gives people a face to associate with the emails in their inboxes.

While a team meeting is an important first step, it's also valuable to have unplanned interactions that mimic the casual encounters employees experience in a typical office environment. Instant messaging is great for this, especially if you can set up a team chat. Take the lead and initiate greetings at the beginning of the day. Start group conversations throughout the workweek— this will help encourage others on the team to do the same. Logging on and starting your day with a round of online hellos and stories about the weekend helps build the sense of belonging to something bigger than just your laptop. Even if it isn't practical for your direct reports to work together on a project, those greetings and conversations can make them feel part of a close-knit team.

Structured fun is another way to create a sense of community for your employees. Find a lull in the workday to get your staff doing something interactive that is non–work related and fun. You may need to try different things, since what one group thinks of as fun may be awkward and uncomfortable for another. If your first efforts don't work out, keep trying. Some people hold game nights, others pair up employees for short conversations (à la speed dating), while still others get the group together and ask each other a set of questions. A little research will yield a workable list of activities to try out: Search online, brainstorm with colleagues, or ask other managers for ideas. While these activities can be awkward at times, they do bring workers together and make them more than colleagues in name only. While some employees might be resistant to this type of interaction, most will appreciate and understand what you're trying to do. You are creating shared experiences.

Building a sense of community is vital, and it isn't hard to do if you go about it intentionally. Even unsuccessful team icebreakers build community—at the very least, they give your direct reports something to talk about among themselves. Take the time to bring your team together as a group and to introduce them to members of the wider company. Your efforts will build a team that is engaged and productive as it interacts with the broader company community.

A Consistent Experience

Change is the new constant, and nowhere is this more true than in the remote workforce. Brick-and-mortar companies are constrained by geography and building leases; remote companies have no such limitations. While this ability to change rapidly can create a company that is agile and resilient, it can also lead to feelings of instability among your direct reports unless you take steps to provide a consistent experience.

Consider what might happen in a traditional office before a large change: Your employees might overhear their colleagues on the other side of the office complaining about a clunky process or program. Or perhaps a series of well-dressed strangers are ushered into the big boss's office. New job descriptions might appear on the company intranet. Even if a large change takes your employees by surprise, most employees upon reflection can realize after the fact that they saw the signs of a change coming. The remote worker, however, doesn't get these same clues. Your employee may not even realize that the company is solving a problem or addressing an opportunity until his work responsibilities change.

While you can't stop the rate of change in your company, you can help your employees weather the storm by providing stability where you can. Keep meeting with your reports on a regular schedule, with a consistent agenda. If you have to create additional points of contact because of the change, make sure your team understands that these are temporary and outside the norm. Your employees should know to expect certain topics to be covered in each meeting so they can prepare. This not only makes the meetings more effective and efficient but also provides a sense of stability when things start changing rapidly.

This doesn't mean that you should run your usual meetings as if nothing has changed. Rather, you should demonstrate that business will carry on, even through the change. Make sure you are as knowledgeable as possible about the upcoming changes. This allows you to speak confidently and firmly with your direct reports. Your employees will take comfort in knowing that their boss understands what's going on and will help them through it. This will allow them to adjust to new processes more smoothly. By the same token, be transparent about what you don't know. Especially when change is large-scale and complex, even senior management may not know for some time exactly how each team will be affected. In the absence of information, employees may suspect that their leadership is hatching some grand plot with nefarious consequences. Reassure your people that the implications of the change are being thought through carefully and information will be shared as soon as possible.

Clarity is also very important. If possible, provide your employees with a clear end date for the old process or structure and show how the new process or structure will work. Make sure that the reasoning around the change is clear to everyone. Without that clarity, speculation will run wild, and virtual employees will be bouncing from one colleague to another, fueling uncertainty and making the experience of working in this fast-paced environment more erratic.

One Monday morning in August 2017, I sat down to work in my home office as usual. I reported to my boss that even though Hurricane Harvey had hit Houston that weekend, my family's house was intact, and I anticipated business as usual that week.

Two hours later, as water rushed down the street and into our neighborhood from a nearby reservoir, I quickly chatted my boss, packed up a few things including my laptop, and headed to higher ground.

The next morning, when I learned that my house had over four feet of water in it (goodbye, recently redone home office), I spent about 15 minutes in shock and then powered up my laptop and started to work. This was the day that I would begin expanding my team to include five new members. I would be the third or fourth manager our new teammates had had in just a few months, so we had a lot to discuss.

I spent that day having individual conversations with each of them to better understand their feelings: anxiety over having a new manager, confusion about the change, and excitement about the opportunities ahead of us.

Over the next several weeks, as I moved from house to house and spent my nights figuring out my next moves, I prioritized my time with my team—not out of a sense of obligation, but because I wanted to do it. Change is one of the most important times to harness strengths, seize the opportunity that comes with new beginnings, and foster engagement. My role in this organizational change was the most important thing to me in those crucial weeks, even as I was personally dealing with some major changes.

—Kate Mitsakis

Proper follow-up is important once changes are announced so you can guide your employees through new initiatives. It will be harder for you to see whether or not your employees are struggling, as you are likely to see only the end result of their work rather than the employees in the process of completing their new tasks. Check in more often with your staff and make sure your regular meetings include a section on dealing with change and new information. Even in the absence of radical change, companies are always updating policies and adjusting operating procedures. If you make these updates a part of your regular meeting agenda, your employees will feel up-to-date instead of lost.

Sometimes the company change is a reorganization, and some or all of your direct reports will soon report to someone else. It may be that the entire team will be broken up and sent in different directions. If this is the case for your team, then there are still things you can do leading up to and throughout this change. You will, of course, want to continue to hold your regular meetings while the team is still engaged in its old work. If you can, help your direct reports get to know their new boss. If you know the new boss prefers instant messaging to email or afternoon meetings to morning ones, for example, share this information. Depending on the circumstances, you may also want to hold one last team-building meeting so your employees can have closure. Your team may continue to work for the same company, but the team itself is going away, and it is important to acknowledge that. Finally, once the changeover has happened, consider sending a brief email or instant message after some time has passed to check in with your former reports. This may not be appropriate in all situations, but this level of human care from an old boss can create a feeling of stability. At its best, reconnecting with former reports underlines for them that change can mean broadening their networks. Change isn't always about loss.

Change is inevitable and necessary. As a manager, you have the power to help your direct reports navigate uncertainty by being a rock of stability. They will look to you, either implicitly or explicitly, to keep the change manageable. If you provide a consistent structure in your interactions with employees, implement steady transitions when change does occur, and focus on well-considered initiatives, you will have a team of people who can survive significant change to their work lives.

A Partner in My Professional Development

At my first annual review, my director walked through my self-selected goals with me, beginning the process of breaking them up into achievable and measurable steps. Then, he gave me an assignment: Make yourself more visible. He explained that knowing colleagues and having them know me was an essential step to growing professionally in the remote environment. While he could and did make some initial connections for me, he pushed me to determine where my greatest interests lie and seek out knowledgeable coworkers on my own. My director can't just make informal introductions for me in the hallway, so he reinforces the importance of my taking the initiative. Of necessity, my development has become more of a conversation than a series of top-down assignments.

—*Caitlin Duke*

In today's business climate, common wisdom says that employees must feel empowered to look for their own professional development opportunities. As a manager who wants to encourage good employees to stick around and grow within the company, it's important that you become a partner in your direct reports' development. This is particularly true for the remote workforce.

In a traditional office, your employees have the opportunity to gain incidental visibility. Perhaps the operations team huddles together every Monday morning near your direct report's desk, where they can observe his fantastic project management skills. Or perhaps your employee happens to be standing in the front office and demonstrates top-notch client support skills when an irate customer comes in the door. Both of these examples have two things in common: The first is that they happen organically. The second is that there is no direct analogue in the remote workforce. Your employees can help out other departments and come to the attention of other managers, but this won't happen unless someone deliberately seeks out those opportunities.

This is where you as a manager can step in. Your position gives you access to people and information that your direct report can't reach on her own. You can be her eyes and ears, uncovering new opportunities to keep her engaged or grow in her career. Not all of these opportunities will pan out, of course, but this is not wasted effort; there is nothing quite so engaging as knowing that your boss is your advocate. Your direct report will appreciate what you're doing to help.

Keep in mind that not all growth opportunities mean helping your employee into a new role. Your employee may not be ready for a next step or even know what that next step ought to be. A side project, either within your department or outside of it, could help her build the skills and visibility she may need to grow into a new role in the future. In some companies, where hierarchies are flat and competition for each role is high, side projects are a great way to "interview" for a role that may open at a later date.

Also consider facilitating one-on-one meetings. In a traditional office, your employee can have lunch with someone whom they find interesting. In the remote workforce, the same connections happen over short one-on-one video calls. These meetings can give your employee the opportunity to connect with someone in an interesting department, to complete business with a cross-functional colleague, or simply to grow by comparing notes with others in a similar role.

Securing growth opportunities for your employees will take time, creativity, and perhaps calling in the occasional favor, so it makes sense to be as efficient as possible. You don't want to set up your direct report with a short stint at the call center, for example, only to find out he was really hoping to learn how to manipulate data with the business intelligence team. Talk to your direct report. You may have a good idea of his strengths and weaknesses in his current role, but you can't assume that you know what he wants to learn next or what activities he may want to explore further. Just because someone is great at a particular task doesn't mean they like doing it.

Be direct and explicit in your conversations with your employee. Does your employee want to grow into a different role? What type of role? What types of experiences does your employee need in order to feel confident applying for that role? Not all employees want to move into different roles. You may be in the enviable position of having an employee who is great at her job and wants to stay in her role indefinitely. In this case she may simply need an occasional side project to keep her from feeling stagnant. Or perhaps she would like to further her skills in a particular program that she uses for her job. You won't know unless you ask.

Remember that answers can change. Just as your company can evolve to meet the needs of the current business climate, your employees' desires can evolve over time. Perhaps the company creates a new department or acquires a business that interests your employee. Or perhaps that side project grows into something more long term, and your report wants to devote more of her work life to it. If you build in regular development checkpoints, you will have an up-to-date grasp of your employee's thinking. This will make you a more effective partner in her development. These development conversations don't have to be long or involved, but many managers find that these talks have to be planned in advance and put on the calendar. Otherwise, it is all too easy to let day-to-day crises push these conversations to a future date that never happens.

If your employees are going to discuss their future career goals with you, they need to feel safe in doing so. Some of your employees may have come from companies with unhealthy cultures. It may be that they think talking about career growth implies that they don't like their current role. The best way to demonstrate that they are in a better place is to talk approvingly of people who took on different projects or reached out for new opportunities. Perhaps you could even share your own development experiences as you encourage your employees to do the same. Your actions will speak for themselves.

Acting as a partner in your employees' professional growth takes time and effort, because it requires that you have a current understanding of their desires and that you invest time in seeking out opportunities to help them grow. However, this is time well spent, yielding engaged employees who will benefit the company for years to come.

Knowing How and Whom to Hire

Not everyone thrives in the remote workforce. It's a matter of personality fit, and no onboarding program—no matter how fantastic—can change a candidate's personality. It's important that candidates who have the best chance of succeeding (not just at the job but also as a remote employee) are the ones who make it to the onboarding stage. Don't assume that someone who applied for a remote job will automatically do well as a remote employee. It's up to you as the hiring manager to ask the right questions in the interview. Otherwise, you'll end up with high turnover and need to put additional time into supporting those who stay but struggle.

While an employee doesn't need to be an expert with technology to be successful in the remote workforce, they do need to have a certain level of tech savvy and be comfortable learning how to work online. As a hiring manager, this is something you should take into account when considering candidates for remote roles. If you bring on someone without first confirming their comfort with technology, you run the risk of having to train them not only on their specific job duties but also on the basics of functioning in the remote environment. There are enough challenges with managing people in the remote workplace without the added trouble of hiring someone who can not or will not learn how to operate in it. When evaluating a candidate's technological skills, it's important to note the difference between posting regularly online versus interacting effectively online. A remote employee should be comfortable with managing email effectively, collaborating on shared documents, and troubleshooting technology at a basic level.

In March of 2015, I began a new position with a daunting objective: develop and launch a nation-wide Ambassador program in five months. I needed my as-yet nonexistent team to get an incredible amount of work done in a short amount of time, and I needed them to do so while working remotely.

This meant being as objective as possible in the interview process and evaluating candidates not only as individuals with different levels of experience, perspective, self-awareness, and capacity for change, but also with the entire group dynamic in mind. To identify the amazing team I needed, I drafted a set of questions that I asked every single candidate in a series of video interviews, meticulously documenting their responses and my observations. I focused on dedication to our mission and vision in addition to the candidates' self-discipline and talents.

In the end, I secured a fantastic team of eight managers and two recruiters who tirelessly worked together toward our common goals. We met via Google Hangouts several times a week, we created group Skype chats for both professional goals and personal bonding, and we were ultimately able to build the trust and relationships we needed. We launched our first training session just four months after I began the hiring process.

—Katie Stanfield

That doesn't mean that you should pass on an otherwise great candidate if they don't already use the specific programs the company uses. Check to see how the candidate has handled past gaps in knowledge. If the candidate has a track record of quickly gaining competency in related areas, then this may be enough to let you proceed with confidence. Of course, keep in mind the amount of time you are willing to spend training new employees.

While being tech savvy is an important selection criterion, a bigger consideration is the candidate's ability to self-direct. Your potential future employee will be on his own at home, trying to get acclimated to a new job and, very likely, a new way of working. While there will undoubtedly be opportunities for your new hire to work closely with you, a trainer, or a colleague, for much of his onboarding, he will be on his own and will need to figure out certain tasks himself. An employee who is more accustomed to an open-plan office environment may struggle to accomplish his work alone in his home office. It will be far harder for someone else to notice when he's struggling or heading down the wrong path, so he'll need to be the type of person who is vocal when he realizes that he needs help. He'll also have to be comfortable looking up solutions and processes, rather than solely relying on asking someone else. Due to the nature of the remote environment, it isn't always possible to find someone who is available to help, so it's important for your new hire to be able to figure some things out on his own. Self-sufficiency, therefore, is key.

Along with the ability to self-direct, a remote employee should have polished people skills and high emotional intelligence. Most interactions will take place via some form of written communication. It takes more emotional intelligence, and not less, to discern tone and intent when communicating with colleagues in this way.

With all this in mind, it's not really enough to conduct a phone interview. You'll need to get as much information about the candidate as possible in order to identify fit, and it's difficult to do this if you can't see the person. You may have candidates who are familiar with making video calls and others who are not. In those cases, it can be a perfect opportunity to find out how they approach learning new skills and how they react to feedback. Just as it's important to do a video interview, it's also important to consider the candidate's email correspondence. If your potential hire is overly casual in his correspondence with you, that could be a red flag, suggesting that he may not understand a level of formality is required in many situations in the remote environment. This could cause problems down the line when interacting with clients or other stakeholders, negatively impacting the business.

The ability to ask the right questions during a job interview and read the candidate well is an important skill for any hiring manager, but you need to take that ability to the next level when hiring someone for the remote workforce. Through careful analysis of video and email interactions, as well as by asking questions about their technical know-how and how they've demonstrated initiative in the past, you can identify those who have the greatest chance of succeeding in both the specific role and the remote environment in general.

Many people are well suited to remote work. If you apply the hard-won knowledge contained within the pages of this book, you will soon wonder how you and your team managed to work any other way.